napa bulletin 16

Insider Anthropology

■ E. L. Cerroni-Long, ed.

National Association for the Practice of Anthropology
A section of the American Anthropological Association

NAPA Bulletins are occasional publications of the National Association for the Practice of Anthropology, a section of the American Anthropological Association.

Ralph J. Bishop and Pamela Amoss
General Editors

Library of Congress Cataloging-in-Publication Data

Insider anthropology / E. L. Cerroni-Long, ed.
p. cm.—(NAPA bulletin ; 16)
Includes bibliographical references.
ISBN 0-913167-72-X
1. Ethnology—Philosophy. 2. Ethnology—Methodology. 3. Ethnology—United States. I. Cerroni-Long, E. L., 1946–. II. Series.
GN345.I375 1995
306'.01—dc20 95-32427
CIP

ISBN 0-913167-72-X

Contents

Introduction: Insider or Native Anthropology?

E. L. Cerroni-Long

Papa Boas would be dumbfounded! After less than a century since the "father of American anthropology" transformed the concept of culture into a key intellectual tool for the understanding of human behavior—and built a new discipline around it—this concept seems to have suffered a fate worse than death. While the term *culture* is now used with both enthusiasm and imprecision by the representatives of the most varied disciplines, by journalists, and by the public at large, many American anthropologists have been mounting a thorough critique of the concept this term defines. Outside the American context, while "cultural anthropology" is still a contested disciplinary designation (a major group of transatlantic practitioners recently named itself the European Association of Social Anthropologists), the hottest intellectual commodity is something called "cultural studies."

This disciplinary hybrid emerged in the 1970s from the rediscovery by British theorists of Gramscian views of "folk" expressions as an emancipatory force. Since then, however, it has shifted ground, so that the concept of class struggle has ceased to be its central point of reference, just as its primary focus has moved away from social structure to subjective identity (Barker and Beezer 1992:16). Thus, by the time it reached the American shores—in the early 1980s—it could easily be grafted onto the main body of anthropological practice, which by that time was largely concerned with related issues of interpretation, subjectivity, and consciousness (see Grossberg et al. 1992).

We have certainly gone a long way from Boas's view of culture as "the genius of a people," and while it is true that the post–World War II world has seen the general establishment of a cultural intellectual paradigm (see Goldschmidt 1985), it is also true that the resolve "to grasping society as a whole, to conceptualizing its underlying principles of unity . . . has passed into crisis" (Dirks et al. 1994:27). The implications of these developments for the applied uses of our discipline are very serious. Should anthropological practice be kept separate from anthropological theory and, especially, from current critical treatments of our discipline's methodological approach? If so, how to disregard the epistemological doubts such critique raises? Even more urgently, how should practicing anthropologists reconcile disciplinary skepticism with the widespread, if superficial, use of basic anthropological terms on the part of their potential clients?

As we struggle with these difficult questions it certainly seems premature to react to the popular appropriation of a vague version of the culture concept by "declaring victory" and setting up camp with the invaders (see Handler 1993). The fact that *culture* is now a popular TV word has not taken us any nearer to a coherent theory of human behavior (Goldschmidt 1985:173), as is clearly illustrated by the ignorance and confusion characterizing current discussions of "multiculturalism" in general and cultural conflict in particular. More worrying, the fact that "it is now commonplace to question whether and in what precise ways culture might be shared (or contested), durable (or constantly changing), coherent and consistent (or inchoate, contradictory, fragmented)" (Dirks et al. 1994:22) may increasingly lead cultural anthropologists to disregard one of the most distinctive aspects of their discipline: its comparative approach.

Erasing Cultural Boundaries

Pointing out that to make comparisons you must have a way of defining what you are comparing is a truism. It is also undeniable, though, that efforts aimed at de-reifying culture end up eliminating an indispensable element of cross-cultural comparisons: cultural boundaries. Without cultural boundaries there is no clear way of defining the relationship of the cultural analyst with the phenomena under observation; consequently, the differentiation between alien and native also disappears, and, as it does, anyone studying a social setting becomes an insider by the mere fact of "being there" to study it.

This turns completely on its head the fundamental methodological premise of classic cultural anthropology: that it is only by becoming immersed for a prolonged period of time into an alien culture that anthropological insights can be gained, to the extent that—to use Srinivas's (1990) phraseology—we become twice-born, as a process of painstaking accumulation of specific observations finally leads us to the recognition of a pattern generalizable to the culture as a whole. At this stage, involving both cognition and emotion, we come to realize that the actions of the people we have studied, once so alien, are perfectly appropriate to the context in which they are performed. Thus we understand that rationality is contextual and not universal, which, in turn, puts into a new perspective our own culturally specific criteria of action. That is why, once we have internalized cultural relativism, going back to studying one's own culture is both difficult—since anthropological insights have forever deprived us of our native naïveté—and very rewarding. If we can train our experientially acquired anthropological lenses on what was once a taken-for-granted reality, we can be born for yet a third time and achieve a level of understanding that goes far beyond both familiarity and empathy, and results in true knowledge.

This was the traditional scenario, and, indeed, up to the mid-1980s, even someone like Clifford Geertz, so crucially influential in setting our discipline on its current postmodern path, would write about the aims of anthropological understanding in terms very compatible to such a scenario (see Geertz 1973, 1983, 1984). What, then, has happened in the last decade? And how is such a momentous change in perspective likely to affect the practicing of anthropology, its applicability, and its relevance?

Actually, 1984 is a date that combines an Orwellian ring with special significance for cultural anthropology. During this year not only was Geertz's American Anthropological Association Distinguished Lecture "Anti Anti-Relativism" published (1984), but a symposium was also organized by the American Ethnological Society specifically to review the "Social Contexts of American Ethnology, 1840–1984" (Helm 1985). Furthermore, that year also saw the publication of a seminal piece of disciplinary self-analysis: Sherry Ortner's "Theory in Anthropology since the Sixties" (1984). This article begins pessimistically, pointing out that the disjunction characterizing anthropology at the beginning of the 1980s could well justify the direst predictions about its future, but it then proceeds to define such disjunction as a "breeding ground for a new and perhaps better order," one likely to become organized around a "new key symbol of theoretical orientation . . . which may be labeled 'practice' (or 'action' or 'praxis')" (Ortner 1984:127). By the end of the article one gets a very clear and satisfying view of how American anthropology has developed all through the 1960s and 1970s, and it is difficult not to share the author's enthusiasm for the "theory of practice" likely to characterize the following decade. The argument advanced, that such a theory uniquely incorporates all three components of the model proposed by Berger and Luckmann (1967)—"that society is a system, that the system is powerfully constraining, and yet that the system can be made and unmade through human action and interaction" (Ortner 1984:159)—appears powerful and truly encouraging. Indeed, a theory of praxis seemed to sociologists to have finally solved the dualistic dilemma caused by the structure/agency contrast; Giddens's influential model of "structuration" depicted a social system in which revolution is preempted by revelation—all the agent needs for changing the system is to be aware both of its characteristics and of the strategic import of individual action.

While Anglo-Saxon sociology went through its "don't worry, be happy" phase, however, only some anthropologists fully embraced praxis theory as their main orientation. Instead, the majority of the American anthropological establishment became increasingly entangled in those webs of significance Clifford Geertz had originally called attention to, and entered a vortex of self-referentiality spiraling toward disciplinary self-destruction. In a way, it could be argued that this end has in fact been reached, if one considers the Boasian concept of culture, the comparative approach, and cultural relativism as the foundations of the discipline. I would argue, though, that this apparently catastrophic outcome may have salutary consequences. Chief among them is the fact that the insider/outsider issue may finally receive the attention it deserves and take central stage in the debate over anthropological practice.

Hybridity and Diversity

In attempting to sort out the process by which our discipline reached its current state it is useful to keep in mind two general points: (1) the historical origin of disciplines profoundly affects their development; and (2) the interaction between theory and methods is circular, so that if theory leads to the selection of particular research methods, those very methods will determine the gathering of results likely to influence both analysis and further theory building. Cultural anthropology is currently being strongly affected both by the long-range implications of interpretive methodological approaches and by the much-delayed repercussions of its rather disreputable origins. To this I would add two other considerations: the recent turn in anthropological theorizing is very congruent with certain fundamental features of the American intellectual tradition, and it fits particularly well with the worldview associated with the phase of capitalistic expansion—variously called postindustrial, consumer, or multinational—presently characterizing most Western societies.

Of all these catalyzing factors, the one perhaps most difficult to grasp is the impact of the interpretive approach. After all, when Geertz suggested that ethnography should be a form of "thick description," he also pointed out that culture, as an "acted document," is public, and that the ethnographer's role is to "inscribe" social discourse (Geertz 1973:Ch. 1). In fact, by calling attention to the role symbols play in perpetuating and circulating culturally specific meanings, he "gave the hitherto elusive concept of culture a relatively fixed focus, and a degree of objectivity, that it did not have before" (Ortner 1984:129). However, by arguing that each culture is "an ensemble of texts, themselves ensembles, which the anthropologist strains to read over the shoulders of those to whom they properly belong" (1973:452), and that "anthropological writings are themselves interpretations" (1973:115), Geertz put a literary metaphor at the center of the anthropological enterprise. This, combined with the ongoing revitalization of literary criticism spurred by deconstructive approaches, had momentous outcomes. On the one hand, it gained cultural anthropology a broader interdisciplinary audience; on the other hand, it also triggered increasing doubts about the validity of anthropological representation (see Clifford and Marcus 1986). Above all, however, and most significantly in terms of the erasure of cultural boundaries, interpretive approaches focused ethnographic research on the analysis of meaning, and since meaning is subjective and polyphonic, a view of culture as disjointed, unbounded, and inchoate accordingly emerged.

Meanwhile, as Foucauldian views of "intellectual discourse" as a vehicle for power and domination kept acquiring popularity all through the 1980s, anthropological reflexivity, already heightened by the interpretive approach, focused ever more critically on the crucial role played by colonialism in the birth and development of our discipline (see Clifford 1988).

This was not a new argument (see Cerroni-Long 1989), but it now acquired new relevance, particularly in reference to the very influential work of Edward Said. In a series of closely argued textual analyses, Said systematically illustrated the process by which cultural differences can be exploited—when they are not altogether invented—to justify colonial domination (see Said 1979, 1983, 1993). While Said's argument remained specifically aimed at tracing the ideological roots of Western "Orientalism," his work, as well as that of a growing number of other Western-based, Third World–born scholars, singled out the category of "the Other" as an invention of Western imperialism and a tool of dominance. Coming from quite a different perspective, a similar argument was also advanced by a growing number of American feminist scholars, and the expanding field of ethnic studies made the critique of "othering" one of its disciplinary foundations.

It is not surprising, therefore, that anthropologists came to be "rightly suspicious of the categories of 'otherness' and 'difference' that have historically been caught in logics of domination and denigration" (Dirks et al. 1994:37). Besides, by jettisoning holistic views of culture, American anthropologists could simultaneously free the discipline from lingering alien influences—such as French structuralism or Marxism—and fall back into the comfortable grooves of a hallowed national tradition. This is a tradition that, in spite of assorted detours caused by external influences, is profoundly rooted in mentalism and personalism. As Harris has often pointed out (1968, 1979), Hume's tough antimetaphysical stance never made much headway within American social science. Similarly, as Varenne has documented (1984), even when American anthropologists talk about culture as the product of social life, their interest and attention is focused either upon the impact this product has on individuals, or on the process by which culture mirrors individual characteristics. An interesting popular reflection of this intellectual outlook is, on the one hand, the profound skepticism most Americans have for the reality of an overarching American culture, and, on the other, the higher tolerance they have for personal idiosyncrasies over group characteristics (Cerroni-Long 1993). In terms of practice, this tradition has led to a rich body of research on values, norms, beliefs, worldviews, personalities, and identities, but to a certain resistance to systemic social theories (Dumont 1986). A view of culture as "the site of multiple contests informed by a diversity of historically specific actions and intentions" (Foster 1991:235) seems a very American view.

It is also a very postmodern view; not only for implying the rejection of all "meta-narratives of human emancipation" (see Lyotard 1984), but also for strikingly reflecting the vision of social life created by consumer capitalism. This is a vision in which the existence of society—understood as a powerfully constraining system with precise structural characteristics—is totally obfuscated by the celebration of the individual mounted by the ever more intrusive media. In turn, this is a direct byproduct of an economy where markets can only be expanded if every individual becomes a consumer and everything becomes a commodity. In such a setting, society is reduced to a "simulacrum" of itself, since it can only be glimpsed through the fictionalized images of it the media feed all of us spectators (Baudrillard 1988). Also, in such a setting, personal identity becomes the ultimate economic frontier, since the range and intensity of individual consumption can only be expanded by breaking the boundaries of the self and convincing the masses to "free" themselves of broad social membership—that is, cultural allegiance—and instead cultivate idiosyncratic diversity or, even better, hybridity. The advertisers' ultimate lure is that, through consumption of different goods, we can invent different selves.

Fredric Jameson (1991) has convincingly documented the correlation between deconstructive approaches in literary criticism and the ideological outlook typical of this third phase of capitalist development; it is not necessary to share his Marxist premises to see how his statements can also help contexualize the current turn in anthropological theorizing. Once we accept the postmodern view of social fragmentation, and cultural boundaries become erased, we can even glorify in the accidents of birth or material conditions that provide us, through our hybrid self, with easy access to multiple realities. This is, in fact, precisely the argument presented by Kirin Narayan in her postmodern take on the insider/outsider debate, provocatively titled "How Native is a 'Native' Anthropologist?" (1993). She complains that "identities are doled out to non-Western, minority, or mixed anthropologists so that exotic difference overshadows commonalities or complexities. That my mother is German-American seems as irrelevant to others' portrayal of me as 'Indian' as the American mothers of the 'Tewa' Alphonso Ortiz, the 'Chicano' Renato Rosaldo, or 'Arab' Lila Abu-Lughod" (1993:677). This is particularly unacceptable since "every anthropologist exhibits . . . a 'multiplex subjectivity.' . . . Which facet of our subjectivity we choose or are forced to accept as a defining identity can change, depending on the context and the prevailing vectors of power" (1993:676). Thus, in her view, the insider/outsider contrast is secondary "to the issue of dismantling objective distance to acknowledge our shared presence in the cultural worlds that we describe. . . . Given the multiplex nature of identity, there will inevitably be certain facets of self that join us up with the people we study, other facets which emphasize our difference" (1993:680). Starting from a similar perspective, another commentator has recently stated: "Anthropology-at-home, for those of us who do not claim to identify exclusively with any country, social class or cultural milieu, holds out a promise that aspects of 'home' will at last be disclosed" (Sciama 1993:14). Interestingly enough, both of the two major collections of Anglo-Saxon "native anthropology" published in recent times have the word *home* in their title (Jackson 1987; Messerschmidt 1981). It could be that this word "privatizes" a half-denied social identity. Or it could be that it reduces cultural membership to emotional familiarity. It remains to be seen, however, what precisely is "home" for people with multiple identities.

Tunnel Vision

That cultural allegiance can not be discounted as glibly as postmodern theorists seem inclined to do is clearly demonstrated by the dramatic recent resurgence of worldwide ethnic conflict. But anthropologists are not in the best position to discuss this phenomenon since they have been particularly remiss at investigating—or even acknowledging—the cultural content of ethnicity. Following Barth's suggestion that the critical focus of investigation should be "the ethnic boundary that defines the group, not the cultural stuff that it encloses" (1969:15) we have spent two decades discussing issues of identity formation and negotiation—again, a mentalist, personalistic approach. And, as postmodernist views of identity took sway, we have subscribed to the "lit crit view" of ethnicity (see Sollors 1986, 1989) and now define it as a "creative process" (see Roosens 1989).

American ethnic studies is a field that provides an ideal focus for the discussion of the insider/outsider issue. As classic cultural anthropology emphasized the need for the "extreme outsider view," ethnic studies ended up expressing an "extreme insider doctrine." Consequently, and in spite of the critique of "othering" developed within the field, it is now generally accepted that only the members of each ethnic group can most effectively study, teach about, discuss, and generally speak for their fellow group members. Obviously, this state of affairs is strongly influenced by political issues of representation and, indeed, by the peculiar popular interpretation of ethnicity that has long been elaborated within American culture (see Cerroni-Long 1986). But in terms of the sociology of knowledge, this is an interesting development. As Robert Merton indicated in a seminal paper, the idea that knowledge is group-specific and that only insiders have access to it has absurd implications: "It would thus seem to follow that only women can understand women—and men men. On the same principle, youth alone is capable of understanding youth, . . . it would then plainly follow that only sociologists are able to understand their fellow sociologists" (1970:13–14). Admittedly, by focusing his discussion on insiders and outsiders—rather than on natives and aliens—and by defining insiders as "the members of specified groups and collectivities or occupants of specified social statuses" (1970:21), Merton can argue that "individuals have not a single status but a status set" (1970:22). Consequently, to suggest that "one must be one in order to understand one" is fallacious since one is not just a woman, or white, or a college graduate, or middle-aged, but may be all of these and more (Merton 1970:24). Certainly, from a philosophical point of view, this is convincing. In fact, if we reject in principle the insiders' monopolistic access to knowledge, Narayan's call for ethnographies simply built upon the acknowledgement of a "shared presence" in the cultural worlds under study seems eminently reasonable. But is it? And are the examples given above for an imaginary Mertonian status-set truly comparable?

The key point is the difference between native and insider. If it is taken seriously, as I think it should, then the previous questions must be answered negatively. It is not just a matter of linguistic quibbling; status-sets involve some that come to us through birth—providing us with native membership—and some which we enter—thus becoming insiders—either by choice or through natural progression through life. Knowledge does not flow automatically from either type of conditions, but access to knowledge does. Furthermore, in the case of memberships entered at birth and continued into adulthood, the learning process involved is so influential that it can only be undone with the greatest difficulty. In the case of culture, the learning touches so many areas of our cognition, emotion, and expression, and in such fundamental ways, that while a person can learn how to survive, or even operate impeccably, in a culture different from the one in which she or he grew up, this "simply adds another layer. . . . It doesn't eliminate what's underneath" (Hall 1979:45). Ethnicity refers to situations in which this layering is established so early and thoroughly that for some members of a culture a particular type of behavioral performance, based on constant code-switching, becomes habitual.

I think it is relevant that while all of these statements go against the grain of the anthropological views of culture and ethnicity that are currently fashionable, they closely match both some of the most common folk attitudes toward the topic, and, especially, the social practice deriving from them. People may cherish cultural hybridity in themselves, but they notice cultural diversity in others, especially when it is group diversity. People may believe that the world is getting homogenized into a huge consumer culture, but they still seek out and join local communities built around some form of cultural similarity, behaviorally expressed. Indeed, as Narayan herself points out, people tend to simplify the complexity of others by focusing on the characteristics that facilitate categorizing them in terms of in-group or out-group membership. Ethnocentrism is alive and well, and de-reifying culture is more likely to feed into it than to assuage it; intellectual positions have all sorts of broader implications, and while they may be developed in good faith they often end up being used in unexpected ways. For example, by "writing out of human history every instance of authentic and autonomous 'Others'," we are also depriving our own political imagination of truly "alternative visions" of social organization (Lee 1993:2). Furthermore, by advancing "invention-of-tradition" arguments, and by denying the relationship between cultural autonomy and nation building, we trivialize the self-definition movements of those very peoples who became the victims of Western colonial domination (Benthall and Knight 1993). At the same time, by failing to acknowledge the impact of cultural and ethnic diversity on interpersonal and intergroup relations we truly abdicate the original aim of our discipline, which was intended as a tool for the amelioration of the human condition. Denying the reality of cultural boundaries implies looking at human transactions through tunnel vision: a limiting perspective caused by the unwillingness to recognize that behavior is shaped by social factors that can only be understood if seen in their appropriate context.

Locating Cultural Knowledge

What, then, can be done to deal constructively with the fact that the disciplinary treatment of fundamental anthropological concepts is diverging ever more dramatically from the way these same concepts are understood and used outside the discipline, often by our potential or actual clients? Can we "reclaim" culture as our integrative theoretical focus? Can we effectively reduce the stereotypical popular perception that anthropology is esoteric and/or irrelevant by contributing to the debate on some of the fundamental issues of our time—multicultural education, ethnic conflict, transnational economic exploitation, electronic conditioning—with approaches that are not abstract, unfeasible, or intellectually patronizing?

I believe we can, and a fundamental first step involves a new attempt at "locating" cultural knowledge. This builds upon the contributions of the last 30 years of anthropological theorizing—including the critique both of a simplistic model of culture and of authoritarian forms of ethnographic representation—but it also goes beyond the paralyzing intellectual impasse created by postmodernism.

Locating cultural knowledge involves a two-pronged approach. First, we need to clarify where it is to be found; second, we need to discuss how it can be retrieved and organized. All of this may seem obvious, but in fact it implies a step-by-step analysis of many disciplinary procedures that are rarely put in the spotlight. Actually, it could be argued that Geertz's approach attracted so much interdisciplinary attention partly because it did spell out, clearly and convincingly, the where and how of the model of anthropological practice it advocated. As mentioned above, this is a model equating cultural knowledge with meaning, to be found in the social discourse of the natives, and retrieved through interpretive—or "thick"—description. If it is true, as many current anthropologists seem to believe, that this approach has now shown its limitations (see Luhrmann 1989), it is not yet clear what is to substitute it.

Some insights on a possible new model—as well as on the shortcomings of the position advocating the dismantlement of the culture concept (e.g., Kahn 1989)—can be derived from a thorough analysis of native anthropology, or rather, native anthropolog*ies*. While rarely discussed or documented in the major disciplinary journals, there are now in the world several well-established traditions of sociocultural anthropology that are strongly culture specific. Their comparative analysis, of which there have been only a few scattered examples so far (Fahim 1982; Hofer 1968; Ishida 1965; Vidyarthi 1979), supports both the popular perception that cultural boundaries do in fact exist and the disciplinarily crucial fact that cultural membership powerfully colors intellectual endeavors, including the study of cultures. Furthermore, comparing native and nonnative anthropological analyses of the same settings permits us to get a better grasp of the type of culture-specific biases that affect both insiders and outsiders. This type of comparison should have by now become a disciplinary routine rather than being exploited from time to time to attack particular authors or to wave the red herring of anthropologists' lack of "objectivity." That cultural knowledge is always partial and situational is not news; from the time Jacques Maquet provided one of the first full-fledged treatments of it the topic has been discussed at many levels, and the conclusion remains the same: "A perspectivist knowledge is not as such nonobjective; it is partial. . . . Nonobjectivity creeps in when the partial aspect is considered as the global one" (Maquet 1964:54). Indeed, it is the arrogance leading many anthropologists to forget this point that some postcolonial critics have rightly attacked (e.g., Appadurai 1988).

Similarly, we should by now be quite aware that the role of anthropological "informants" has always been much more crucial than most classic ethnographies reveal (Sanjek 1993). If current critiques of representation have stimulated the recognition of the fundamentally cooperative character of ethnography, this is a positive result. And if such recognition leads to imaginative ways of providing a channel for the native voice itself (e.g., see Bernard and Salinas Pedraza 1989), it is even better. However, in the newfound enthusiasm for the native point of view, we should not forget that it is still a point of view, and even dialogic attempts simply produce another, dialogic point of view. It is perhaps useful to consider that if cultural knowledge is in the natives it may be so internalized and "tacit" (Polanyi 1966) that it remains knowledge without understanding. The nonnative anthropologist, on the other hand, may well reach understanding but can never acquire true knowledge, the same way that a woman may fully understand what it is like to be a man but cannot quite know, and vice versa. That is where native anthropology may provide the ultimate form of "insider knowledge." We definitely need more of it, but we also need to assess whether it is in fact built upon true insider knowledge, and this can best be achieved through systematic comparisons of native/nonnative ethnographies.

Another reason why analyzing native anthropology is important is that it prods one to consider in which way our discipline differs from other social sciences, particularly sociology. If anthropologists are not just comparative sociologists, what are they? The answer to this question actually provides the other half of the locating-knowledge puzzle. Once you have clarified where cultural knowledge is, you still need to figure out how to retrieve it. This has a lot to do with methodology—and let us remember that methods always affect results—but, more basically, it also has to do with scope. The scope of Boasian cultural anthropology was holistic, in the sense that it aimed at finding, illustrating, and analyzing the network of connections sustaining and channeling human behavior. These were connections with the biological characteristics of our species and with our habitats, but they were also the internal connections linking various aspects of the culture, be they social, psychological, or expressive. That is precisely why the Boasian version of the culture concept became central to the discipline, since it illustrated a research scope much broader than the one sociologists, economists, political scientists, historians, or even psychologists could claim. If we jettison the culture concept we lose this scope, and with it the unique point of view on the human condition that our discipline can contribute, and which makes it so relevant to the solution of real-life problems. What I suggest, then, is that the "how" question be answered both by clearly describing our methodological choices, and by organizing the results obtained through their application in a way aimed at highlighting their multiple connections. Again, this can best be achieved through a creative use of insider knowledge.

Inside American Culture

A true insider anthropology, then, is a reflexive form of native anthropology, implying so much more than simply "practicing at home." It means that it is done on the basis of constant reflection upon one's biases to discern whether they may be personal or culture specific. It means that results are specifically offered for inspection to both the fellow natives under study and cultural outsiders. It means that it is built upon cross-cultural expertise on how the problem under study has been addressed in different cultural settings. It means that it incorporates systematic comparisons of native and nonnative research. It means that it clearly locates cultural knowledge both in terms of "where" it is and of "how" it should be retrieved and organized. It means, above all, that an attempt is made at developing a "theory of practice," by assessing the cultural matrices of research interests, ways of defining research problems, and approaches to their solution. This, I believe, is precisely what Bourdieu calls "participant objectivation" (Wacquant 1989:33) and defines as the foundation of a "logic of practice" (Bourdieu 1990).

The way natives describe their culture is characterized by a specific choice of what aspects of it do or do not deserve discussion, and of how observations should be used and interpreted. This choice, if challenged, often cannot be easily explained (see Reddy 1993). The reflexive native anthropologist, however, is uniquely positioned to investigate how these almost automatic choices relate to the overall cultural pattern from which they emerge. This process is not very different from what Berreman long ago called "ethnography of ethnography" (1966). However, if theories of culture are culturally determined, it is crucial that the ethnography of ethnography be done in the context of the researcher's own culture (see Kapferer 1990; Kuper 1992). In most cases this process can only be initiated after studying other cultures and deliberately "distancing" oneself from the natives

(Ohnuki-Tierney 1984; see also Fowler and Hardesty 1994), but its outcome is so promising that it justifies the preparation required.

This collection of articles includes a variety of examples of insider anthropology, from informal reflections on research and application to full-fledged case studies of reflexive analysis. The one conclusion all of the authors reach, albeit through different routes, is that to do real insider anthropology requires grappling with issues of power. The final piece, by Barbara Pillsbury, spells this out most forcefully by discussing the difficulties involved in translating for "native consumption" the lessons learned through the implementation of social reform programs in foreign cultural settings. American interest in speeding up the "economic development" of "third world" countries often leads to linking various forms of financial aid with the implementation of progressive social programs, often designed and administered by anthropologists. At home, on the other hand, the holistic anthropological perspective is likely to be politically awkward, and the carrot of financial aid is simply unavailable. In the complex play of international relations anthropological input may be considered useful for addressing foreign social problems, but not domestic ones.

The intrusion of "political" factors in the definition of what is appropriate—indeed, even available—for anthropological analysis has long been recognized, but this issue acquires special significance when considered in reference to native research. Mari Womack points this out in her piece, which discusses the social implications of cultural relativism. Is the glorification of an alien culture's exotic characteristics a proper application of relativism? Are anthropologists supposed to "award a stamp of approval" to any group they study, or is this usually done simply because the groups most often studied are marginal and powerless, and anthropologists feel paternalistic toward them? To do insider anthropology while studying areas of one's own culture defined by the rich and powerful is a great challenge; the aura of power is seductive enough to entice the type of emotional involvement that impairs methodological relativism. Ironically, it is precisely methodological relativism, reflexively applied, that can help us maintain detachment.

While both studying down and studying up may create specific forms of bias, the most problematic situation arises when an anthropologist attempts to study a social group she or he consciously identifies with. Both Jaffe and Jones address this issue by describing how their respective research projects catalyzed a complex process of self-reflection, which ultimately greatly affected the projects themselves. In Jaffe's case the result was the realization that serving in the military critically limited her capacity to do an ethnography of it. In Jones's case it was a reconsideration of the meaning of social advocacy for a black intellectual studying a black social enclave characterized by internal conflict.

Advocacy, of course, has directly to do with power, but it has also to do with the status and role a society assigns to intellectuals in general and social scientists in particular. Reflexive native analysis may bring these assumption to the fore and, as Jones describes, may lead one to take a stand about them. For practicing anthropologists, however, the situation is further complicated by the expectations of our clients, and by the conflict that may arise between fulfilling one's contractual obligations and playing out an advocacy role. Liebow's article addresses this issue and presents some suggestions on how to successfully deal with the moral dilemmas created by maintaining an outsider position while doing insider research.

This is not just a question of balancing emics and etics, as all anthropologists must do (Lett 1990). Rather, it involves sorting out—and subtly counteracting—the process by which the institutionalization of decision making ends up privileging particular groups as the only legitimate "fact bearers." As Liebow points out, this can only be achieved by retrieving all the locally held knowledge—both expert and lay—and by applying it to the solution of the problems our clients hire us to address. This means having the ability to act as "cultural mediators" by effectively translating potentially dissonant information so that it can be constructively used in the decision-making process. In turn, this requires that we detect the "unfamiliar in the familiar" just as often as we do the opposite.

As Goldschmidt argues in his article, doing native research necessitates fine tuning our approach, both to correctly identify what to focus attention on and to decide how to present one's findings. As one starts training the anthropological lens on the familiar one discovers that the social dimension of "facts" is a concretion of different, often conflicting, interpretations. These interpretations are organized into "myths" that provide a blueprint for the corporate behavior of specific social groups. Yet these myths are also constantly open to transformation, as the "facts" they are built upon get reinterpreted through social practice.

The characteristics of insider anthropology give us an opportunity to further catalyze this process by injecting social practice with the results of our research. In this sense, our work has an intrinsic applied component, and we are agents of sociocultural change whether we like it or not. This realization should in itself assuage some of the disciplinary self-doubts brought about by the postmodern perspective. It should also give a new impetus to a type of research which is still all too rare.

It has been said that anthropologists "have done more research in the United States in the last dozen years than in the entire previous history of the discipline" (Moffatt 1992:205). I would argue that not much of it qualifies as true insider anthropology in the sense discussed here. In fact, most of the recent studies of American culture done by anthropologists are indistinguishable on the one hand from classic outsider research or, on the other, from good qualitative sociology—or even investigative journalism. This may be partly caused by the postmodern malaise: the disorientation that comes from the erasure of cultural boundaries. Or it may derive from the fact that researchers have naively adopted popular attitudes toward cultural denial and subcultural autonomy. In any case, very few recent studies of American culture address from the inside, reflexively and holistically, some of its most problematic aspects, such as ethnic conflict, imbalanced power allocation, privileged enclaves, or self-destructive social practices.

The articles collected here do this. Thus they provide successful attempts, I believe, at a true "repatriation" of American anthropology (see Rappaport 1993). They also illustrate a realization that should be crucial to popularizing our disciplinary contribution: "The ignorance with which anthropology is faced is not 'folly' to be corrected, still less a void to be filled, but the very human condition of unreflection to be challenged" (Knight 1993:2).

Notes

Acknowledgments. The idea for this collection emerged from organizing and chairing the symposium "Cross-Cultural Perspectives on Native Anthropology" for the XII International Congress of Anthropological and Ethnological Sciences, held in Zagreb, Yugoslavia, in summer 1988. Very early versions of some of the articles collected here were in fact first presented at that symposium. Since then I have been exchanging ideas on native anthropology not only with each of the contributors but also with a large number of American and international scholars whose work could not be represented here. I sincerely thank them all but I want to single out M. N. Srinivas, who patiently wrote up and shared with me some of his most recent ideas on "insider anthropology" and, when invited to include them in this collection, declined in favor of publishing in India, gently explaining that the whole point of insider research is to make sure that fellow insiders get to read it!

References Cited

Appadurai, Arjun
1988 Putting Hierarchy in Its Place. Cultural Anthropology 3:36–47.
Barker, Martin, and Anne Beezer
1992 Introduction: What's in a Text? *In* Reading into Cultural Studies. Martin Parker and Anne Beezer, eds. Pp. 1–20. New York: Routledge.
Barth, Fredrik
1969 Introduction. *In* Ethnic Groups and Boundaries. Fredrik Barth, ed. Pp. 9–38. Boston: Little, Brown.
Baudrillard, Jean
1988 Selected Writings. Stanford, CA: Stanford University Press.
Benthall, Jonathan, and John Knight
1993 Ethnic Alleys and Avenues. Anthropology Today 9(5):1–2.
Berger, Peter, and Thomas Luckmann
1967 The Social Construction of Reality. Garden City, NY: Doubleday.
Bernard, H. Russell, and Jesus Salinas Pedraza
1989 Native Ethnography: A Mexican Indian Describes His Culture. Newbury Park, CA: Sage.
Berreman, Gerald D.
1966 Anemic and Emetic Analyses in Social Anthropology. American Anthropologist 68:346–354.
Bourdieu, Pierre
1990 In Other Words. Stanford, CA: Stanford University Press.
Cerroni-Long, E. L.
1986 Ideology and Ethnicity: An American-Soviet Comparison. Journal of Ethnic Studies 14(3):1–29.

1989 Child of Colonialism: The Primitivist Premises of Western Anthropology. North Dakota Quarterly 57(3):76–98.
1993 Cultural Denial: American Identity in the Age of Multiculturalism. Paper presented at the annual meeting of the American Anthropological Association, Washington, DC, November 17.
Clifford, James
1988 The Predicament of Culture. Cambridge, MA: Harvard University Press.
Clifford, James, and George E. Marcus, eds.
1986 Writing Culture. Berkeley: University of California Press.
Dirks, Nicholas B., Geoff Eley, and Sherry B. Ortner, eds.
1994 Culture/Power/History. Princeton: Princeton University Press.
Dumont, Louis
1986 Essays on Individualism. Chicago: University of Chicago Press.
Fahim, Hussein, ed.
1982 Indigenous Anthropology in Non-Western Countries. Durham, NC: Carolina Academic Press.
Foster, Robert J.
1991 Making National Cultures in the Global Ecumene. Annual Review of Anthropology 20:235–260.
Fowler, Don D., and Donald L. Hardesty, eds.
1994 Others Knowing Others. Washington, DC: Smithsonian Institution Press.
Geertz, Clifford
1973 The Interpretation of Cultures. New York: Basic Books.
1983 Local Knowledge. New York: Basic Books.
1984 Distinguished Lecture: Anti Anti-Relativism. American Anthropologist 86:263–278.
Goldschmidt, Walter
1985 The Cultural Paradigm in the Post-War Period. *In* Social Contexts of American Ethnology, 1840–1984. June Helm, ed. Pp. 164–176. Washington, DC: American Anthropological Association.
Grossberg, Lawrence, Cary Nelson, and Paula A. Treichler, eds.
1992 Cultural Studies. New York: Routledge.
Hall, Edward T.
1979 Learning the Arabs' Silent Language. Interview with Kenneth Friedman. Psychology Today 13(3):45–54.
Handler, Richard
1993 Anthropology Is Dead! Long Live Anthropology! American Anthropologist 95:991–995.
Harris, Marvin
1968 The Rise of Anthropological Theory. New York: Crowell.
1979 Cultural Materialism. New York: Random House.
Helm, June, ed.
1985 Social Contexts of American Ethnology: 1840–1940. Washington, DC: American Anthropological Association.
Hofer, Tamas
1968 Comparative Notes on the Professional Personality of Two Disciplines. Current Anthropology 9(4):311–315.
Ishida, Eiichiro
1965 European vs. American Anthropology. Current Anthropology 6(3):303–318.
Jackson, Anthony, ed.
1987 Anthropology at Home. London: Tavistock.
Jameson, Fredric
1991 Postmodernism, or, the Cultural Logic of Late Capitalism. Durham, NC: Duke University Press.
Kahn, Joel
1989 Culture: Demise or Resurrection? Critique of Anthropology 9(2):5–25.
Kapferer, Bruce
1990 From the Periphery to the Centre. *In* Localizing Strategies. Richard Fardon, ed. Pp. 280–302. Washington, DC: Smithsonian Institution Press.
Knight, John
1993 On Public Ignorance. Anthropology Today 9(2):1–2.

Kuper, Adam, ed.
1992 Conceptualizing Society. New York: Routledge.
Lee, Richard
1993 The Primitive as Problematic. Anthropology Today 9(6):1–3.
Lett, James
1990 Emics and Etics: Notes on the Epistemology of Anthropology. *In* Emics and Etics. Thomas N. Headland, Kenneth L. Pike, and Marvin Harris, eds. Pp. 127–142. Newbury Park, CA: Sage.
Luhrmann, T. M.
1989 Anthropology and Autobiography (part 2). Anthropology Today 5(4):27–28.
Lyotard, Jean-Francois
1984 The Postmodern Condition. Minneapolis: University of Minnesota Press.
Maquet, Jacques J.
1964 Objectivity in Anthropology. Current Anthropology 5(1):47–55.
Merton, Robert K.
1970 Insiders and Outsiders: A Chapter in the Sociology of Knowledge. American Journal of Sociology 78(1):9–47.
Messerschmidt, Donald A., ed.
1981 Anthropologists at Home in North America. New York: Cambridge University Press.
Moffatt, Michael
1992 Ethnographic Writing about American Culture. Annual Review of Anthropology 21:205–229.
Narayan, Kirin
1993 How Native is a "Native" Anthropologist? American Anthropologist 95:671–686.
Ohnuki-Tierney, Emiko
1984 "Native" Anthropologists. American Ethnologist 11:584–586.
Ortner, Sherry B.
1984 Theory in Anthropology since the Sixties. Comparative Studies in Society and History 26(1):126–166.
Polanyi, Michael
1966 The Tacit Dimension. New York: Doubleday.
Rappaport, Roy A.
1993 Distinguished Lecture in General Anthropology: The Anthropology of Trouble. American Anthropologist 95:295–303.
Reddy, Prakash G.
1993 Danes Are Like That. Mfrke, Denmark: Grevas Forlag.
Roosens, Eugeen E.
1989 Creating Ethnicity. Newbury Park, CA: Sage.
Said, Edward W.
1979 Orientalism. New York: Vintage Books.
1983 The World, the Text, and the Critic. Cambridge, MA: Harvard University Press.
1993 Culture and Imperialism. New York: Knopf.
Sanjek, Roger
1993 Anthropology's Hidden Colonialism. Anthropology Today 9(2):13–18.
Sciama, Lidia
1993 Aspects of Home. Times Literary Supplement, July 16, 14.
Sollors, Werner
1986 Beyond Ethnicity. New York: Oxford University Press.
1989 The Invention of Ethnicity. *In* The Invention of Ethnicity. Werner Sollors, ed. Pp. ix–xx. New York: Oxford University Press.
Srinivas, M. N.
1990 Caste in Modern India and Other Essays. Bombay: Media.
Varenne, Herve
1984 Collective Representations in American Anthropological Conversations: Individual and Culture. Current Anthropology 25(3):281–299.
Vidyarthi, L. P.
1979 Trends in World Anthropology. Delhi, India: Concept Publishing Company.
Wacquant, Loic J. D.
1989 Toward a Reflexive Sociology. Sociological Theory 7(1):26–63.

The Unfamiliar in the Familiar

Walter Goldschmidt

Can people really study their own culture? Is what they study their own culture or some alien subculture within their own society? Is not an essential element of the cultural perspective a disengagement from one's own culture—alienation? These questions are at the center of this article.

My technical qualifications for discussing "native anthropology" derive from the study I made of California rural communities in the early forties. I had best start by describing how I happened to get into this activity. I had already formulated, dimly and awkwardly to be sure, the central concerns that have dominated my thinking throughout my career; namely, the interrelationship of three matters: society as a structure, culture as a set of values, and the individual as a motivated actor. It was hard in those years to get funding for research, but I learned about a source for the study of a California community and finally obtained a munificent grant of $1,000 from M. L. Wilson, an "old westerner" who ran the Agricultural Extension Service. He agreed to support the research by saying, "Yes, yes, I want you to round up the culture!" and made a gesture I never forgot, a circular arm movement as if herding dogies into a corral.

So I went to Wasco in 1940. It was a town of about 5,000 people, surrounded by farms mostly of moderate size that had been pioneered just before World War I, when pump irrigation was new. By 1940 the farmers were fairly prosperous, growing potatoes, cotton, and tomatoes; there were orchards and a little dairying. Most farmers specialized in one of the crops. Their operations were heavily mechanized, and they required masses of seasonal labor—migrant workers. Some of these workers—Mexicans, Blacks, and Okies—were settled in Wasco and "followed the crops" for seasonal work elsewhere, while others came to Wasco when labor was at peak demand there. Wasco itself was a shopping and trade center; most of the elite were local representatives of corporations: oil companies, supply outfits, the bank, and the like. The town was unincorporated at the time and had no political organization; the president of the local branch of the Bank of America was referred to as the "unofficial mayor." Farmers and farmers' wives participated in local community affairs, especially in the churches and the social clubs, but as they were busy, they were less active in these matters than were the corporate representatives, whose participation was actually an important part of their work. I called this elite of professionals, executive, and farmers the "nuclear group."

Farm laborers were excluded from most community affairs, and even regularly hired men rarely joined together with nuclear group members in any activity. Thus the social organization can be characterized as being made up of two classes with an almost impenetrable barrier between them: one in control of the community and the other excluded from participation. They lived together peaceably enough while I was there, but that was because bitter battles over unionization had taken place a few years before, and the power of the state along with local forces had effectively subordinated and disenfranchised the workers.

Was I studying my own culture? I come from a German-American background in San Antonio, raised in what we irreverently called "Sauerkraut Bend." One of my childhood memories is that when I came home from school and went out to play after raiding the icebox, I joined my two best friends—a Mexican American who had something concocted of frijoles (which I secretly coveted) and an Irish boy with a peanut butter sandwich, while I had schmirkase or leberwurst on my pumpernickel. Thus I was aware early, and I might add consciously and without prejudice, of subcultural variations while still in grammar school. This prepared me for life as an anthropologist, but it hardly suggests that Wasco was representative of my culture. It was no less alien and far more frightening than any of the exotic peoples I have studied since.

Of course, in a broader sense, Wasco was part of my culture, and this had two major effects, one advantageous and the other a source of problems. The great advantage is in the matter of language. I have not myself been able to work elsewhere in the vernacular, and while I see this as a weakness on my part, I remain skeptical as to how full any anthropologist's competence is in the language of his subjects, in view of the generally low competence displayed in their own. To be fully conversant with one's informants' utterances, the nuances of their meanings, and the assumptions underlying these meanings is a very great help in understanding what is going on and what is in their minds. One also has the advantage of knowing the basic institutions.

The disadvantage is in having to deal with the familiar—and the familiar is so familiar that you don't know what to say. What is news to your audience? Obviously, one does not describe the automobiles or the kitchen gadgets or what a high school is. The problem is to select from the vast array of events that appear before one's eyes those things that are relevant. To be sure, all ethnographers select; all edit their observations, but in dealing with one's own culture, there is a tremendous amount of selecting out—and this is not easy.

The answer is to find the unfamiliar within the familiar, to make it clear that things are not what they seem, to reach behind the facade of ordinary behavior and belief to the deeper implications of social action. In the remainder of this article I want to show the conflict between the inner reality of beliefs and institutions and the external expression of them.

I was concerned, then, with understanding the values and the status system in a community that had been impacted over the preceding decade by the immigration of white agriculture laborers who had taken over much of the field work that for nearly a century had been done by ethnic minorities. In the America of the thirties public opinion was quite explicit that Asians—Chinese, Japanese, and Filipino—were by nature suited to stoop labor—and implicitly only to stoop labor. (The leading textbook on agricultural economics of the time explicitly stated that field labor could only be done by those races whose short legs and lack of intelligence naturally endowed them for such work.) I am certain that most of the people that constituted the nuclear group of Wasco really believed this convenient myth. But they blandly applied these racist notions to the impoverished Anglo-Saxon types, the blond, blue-eyed people from the Ozarks, from Oklahoma, Arkansas, and Texas. It should have created cognitive dissonance, but when people are sufficiently imbued with ideas that are convenient and comfortable to their social position they simply do not see reality. This is my first example of seeing the unfamiliar in the familiar.

Consider next the schools. Everybody knows that schools are created to educate the young, to teach them the three R's, a few myths about our government and history, and bowdlerized versions of Shakespeare and other classics. Everybody knows that schools are a means of selecting individuals on the basis of their learning ability to fill positions of responsibility in accordance with their level of capability. These are what Merton would call the manifest function of schools. The latent functions are something quite different. The high school was a major source of civic pride, a community icon, a temple. It had an auditorium, which could serve the congregation of the town as a town, but that was far less important to the people than that it had a football team to represent it in competition with rival towns. That aspect of the school was more important sociologically. While the education system, with its constant testing and grading, is designed to discriminate on the basis of intellectual capacity between those who are to go on to be leaders and those who are not, the school did in fact do the opposite; it was the one institution that served to unify the community, where blacks and Okies and Chicanos could be together with the elite. I am not suggesting that discrimination was absent, that blacks and whites dated, but that at least from time to time they sat down to eat lunch together and had some contact. There was, for instance, the case of the successful Okie football player who, after early rebuffs, came to be accepted at parties given by the upper-status students as a result of his athletic prowess.

If the institution that should have been differentiating was the single source of unity, the institution that should have been unifying was quite the opposite. Though in the eyes of God, according to the Christian doctrine (no non-Christian religious institution existed then in Wasco), all are equal, the churches in Wasco were bastions of social discrimination. There was one Catholic Church, but it had separate masses for Mexicans and Anglos;

the priest told me that the Mexicans were more primitive and liked mass to be more colorful. Most of Wasco was Protestant; there were nine Protestant churches for whites in the community and two, fully segregated, for blacks (who were segregated geographically as well). I asked the minister of the most prestigious church what would happen if a black asked to join his congregation. As it happens, this was a Congregational church, which, if you know your church history, is very liberal. The idea intrigued him; he first said that there would have to be some "reason" (presumably that the applicant had the appropriate socioeconomic status), which already tells us something, and then that he would put the matter before his board of deacons. "I think," he said, and I could see that he was counting the votes, "it would be approved. It would be all over town anyway, whatever was decided."

Because racial discrimination was so obvious and open throughout the United States at the time, I found more interest in the status distinctions within the white population. The nine churches were like a layer cake, divided into four levels:

- The elite church (already mentioned) with a congregation made up of 81 percent managers, professionals, and farmers, and only 19 percent laboring class (none of whom were migratory workers)
- A middle group in which the ratio was about 50-50
- A lower-middle group with a ratio of about 40-60
- The schismatic Pentecostal congregation, where all members but one were migrant farm workers

Though worshipping the same words of God, church rituals varied widely. At the Congregational ceremony (and to a lesser extent at the Baptists' and Methodists') it was very sedate and elegant, the congregation well dressed, the service quiet and the sermon innocuous. At the third-level churches the sermons were more volatile, the appeal more emotional and filled with fire and brimstone, with emphasis given to the punishments and rewards in the afterlife. In the schismatic church the lay preacher gave a sermon that was directly inspired by God; he shouted imprecations and warnings and appealed to the repressed emotions of his congregation. The flock, in turn, also entered into the spirit of the affair, or, more in accord with their perceptions, the spirit entered them: many entered into a trance state, "talking in tongues" and rolling on the floor, confessing sins and appealing to the congregation for support. This ritual was a public assertion of the sinfulness of the world and the ultimate importance of faith. It was an assertion that the true believers were first in the eyes of God, that their reward would come in Heaven when the elite would suffer eternal damnation.

We see in these activities how the single Christian religion was bent to meet the needs of persons of different stations in the community, how the religious performance was shaped to meet the variant emotional needs of these several social strata, and that in the process the institution of the church served as a means of maintaining and reinforcing the status system of Wasco.

My final example is the clubs and social organizations of Wasco. There were 12 such groups—fraternal orders, service and special interest, and women's clubs. These organizations had the explicit function of supplying recreational social life and promoting community welfare. They were expected to be apolitical and nondiscriminatory. Of the approximately 700 persons of known occupation (for women, the occupation of their husbands if they were not in the work force) belonging to these clubs, only about 35 percent were unskilled workers, while over 60 percent were businessmen, professionals, or farm operators. Business and professional people were more than twice as active as the farmers. If either blacks or Mexicans were among these memberships, I did not hear of it.

These clubs were, in fact, arenas of political action. It was through these organizations, especially the service clubs, that political decisions were made. When local issues were raised, such as what to do about the pauper cemetery or whether the town should be incorporated, these were effectively decided by votes taken in these clubs. When the county authorities sought "community sentiment," they would ask the clubs to put it on their agenda, for to them it was these groups that constituted the community. We must remember that not only were these clubs entirely in the hands of the elite but also that this elite was not really made up of local people. The great majority were representatives of such corporations as the Union Oil Company, Bank of America (then the largest chain bank in California), Pacific Gas and Electric Company, and the like. That meant that their position on such matters was congruent with, if not actually dictated by, the corporations to which they owed their loyalty and their livelihood.

When we examine our own culture, we learn that things are not what they seem. This is an important lesson in its own right, but it also leads us to examine that which underlines the apparent reality, the pretended reality of the community. We uncover the fact that there are pervasive myths that are extremely convenient to the participants: the myth of race, the myth of community, the myth of participatory democracy, the myth of religious equality and the theological basis for the social order. In Wasco even those most disadvantaged by the system, the impoverished Okies, formulated a myth that helped to make their lot bearable.

Don't misunderstand me: these ideas were, I am certain, truly believed by most of the participants and vaguely accepted by the remainder; they were not the product of some cynical scheme. There is one further lesson in this. If this mythical world can be created by members of complex, "developed" societies, might it not also be the case that the mythical world of tribal peoples, so assiduously studied by anthropologists, is also just a convenient set of beliefs, as separate from the reality in which they actually operate as was the mythology I found in Wasco?

Inside the Decision-Making Process: Ethnography and Environmental Risk Management

Edward Liebow

An icy blast of February air rushed by as I stepped from my rented Mazda onto the gravel driveway. I looked at my watch. Right on time, I noted, and I patted my coat's outer pocket. I was feeling for my keys before closing the car door. The wind swirling over this frozen crust of eastern Washington farmland was perfumed with spearmint, a reminder that my host was one of the largest producers of mint oil in North America. He was also the leader of a group of local agribusiness people staunchly opposed to siting a privately operated hazardous waste incinerator nearby. It was 1989, and times were tough all over rural America. For most crops, production and prices paid to farmers had peaked in the early 1980s but declined over the latter part of the decade. Agricultural land values in eastern Washington state also declined throughout the 1980s, mirroring a wider national trend. The year before, a highly publicized controversy over Alar, a chemical used on some types of red apples, had devastated growers in the region, who had been looking forward to their first good crop in several years. To adjust to changing market conditions, local growers were contemplating a shift to crops earning more per acre, but changes in crop inventory are almost always accompanied by increased financial uncertainty. The uncertain potential of market effects from a hazardous waste incinerator—a decreased demand for locally produced crops due to possible contamination—loomed as an unwelcome addition. Feeling a key in my coat, I slammed shut the driver's door, and only too late caught a glimpse of a key in the ignition switch. My car keys were safely in my coat, but the rental car keys were now locked inside. My host's wife must have been watching from the mint distillery's office window; she walked briskly out the door, failing to contain her laughter or her energetic golden retrievers. "You must be Ed," she said, as she tried to call off the dogs. "Take the Cadillac into town. The keys are in it. To the sheriff's office. I phoned, but he said he was too busy to come out just now. He has one of those 'slim-jims.' You can use it. My husband has gone off to help a neighbor, but he should be back about the time you are."

What a way to start a month of interviews! Let me assure you, this article is not from the "tales from the field" genre, filled with accounts of embarrassments I've endured as a fieldworker. Rather, much of my recent work concerns how local knowledge may inform environmental risk management decisions (e.g., Liebow 1988, 1993; Liebow et al. 1993; Liebow and Wolfe 1993). This work relies on insights offered by a number of scholars who argue that our views of what constitute environmental hazards worth worrying about are situated in a more encompassing scheme of social organization and value orientations (see Douglas 1985, 1992; Douglas and Wildavsky 1982; Rappaport 1988; Rayner and Cantor 1987). From this viewpoint, culturally patterned orientations toward equity, consent, trust, liability, and time may be of particular relevance to the selection and evaluation of environmental hazards. If I hadn't already been tipped off in arranging this series of interviews, the incident stemming from the rental car keys should have certainly clued me in that this was different "trust" territory. The rural county sheriff handing a perfect stranger his device for breaking into locked cars, solely on a friend's word; a neighbor's need put before an appointment with a stranger—this certainly wasn't Seattle.

In this article I want to pick up on one of the central themes Cerroni-Long articulates in her introductory piece—locating cultural knowledge. Reducing the risk of environmental hazard from potentially dangerous technologies involves value-laden, frequently conflict-riddled, choices over where local burdens should be created to achieve a widespread benefit: the incinerator that removes the threat of hazardous wastes infiltrating a whole region's drinking water supply has to be in someone's backyard, as does the reactor that produces radiological isotopes used to diagnose and treat grave illnesses. In practical terms, the issue here is deciding who has seats at the table where these choices get made; in other words, what qualifies as applicable knowledge and insight? Too often the question of who is qualified to make decisions about the distribution of environmental risk and uncertainty is decided by risk managers and technical specialists (distinguished by their advanced training in the analysis of environmental, health, and safety hazards). On the strength of their training, risk managers and specialists tend to set themselves apart from laypersons, whose specialized knowledge does not encompass this domain. In addition to labeling laypersons "inexpert," risk managers and specialists tend to discount laypersons' judgments as ill informed, politically motivated, or both. Having discounted laypersons' judgments, managers/specialists can then proceed to exclude laypersons from risk management decisions. As I have noted elsewhere (Liebow 1993), among the more disabling effects of being excluded from these decisions are (1) a lack of trust in the risk managers and (2) a felt lack of control over the potential hazards' sources. Research has amply demonstrated that these effects, in turn, are likely to elevate, rather than reduce, the hazards' judged riskiness in the view of those who have been excluded from the table where decisions are being made. One specific aim of the practice of anthropology in environmental planning is to give voice to the knowledge and insights of nonspecialists, whose experience, often with a series of highly relevant events, lends authority to lay judgments about environmental dangers and the public agencies responsible for managing those dangers.

The remaining sections of this article review what I consider a disabling dichotomy between "experts" and "laypersons" and the role that cultural knowledge plays in structuring risk management problems. To illustrate this discussion I will draw examples primarily from the incinerator study and also from my involvement with interactions between the U.S. Department of Energy and the Native American tribes of the Pacific Northwest. In my earlier commentary on this subject (Liebow 1993) I concluded with some prescriptive advice to risk managers on how to "open up" the decision-making process, acknowledging native expertise as credible and making a sincere effort to understand the social setting from which disparate domains of expertise originate. Here I conclude with a bit of advice about applying ethnographic research by seeking a vantage point from "inside" the decision-making process to help ensure the avoidance or reduction of potential environmental hazards. This echoes an appeal made by Laura Nader (1974) more than 20 years ago about the necessity for "studying up."

The Expert/Layperson Dichotomy

In the view of those who control risk management policy making, two propositions inform the dichotomy between experts and laypersons:

- Experts base their conclusions on statistical reasoning, while laypersons do not
- Other principles of reasoning (beside statistical) do not apply to the evaluation of hazards (Brown 1987, 1992)

In the starkest terms, laypersons are said to use an "intuitive" approach to risk judgment (focusing on the controllability of hazards and their catastrophic consequences), in contrast with the "analytical" approach used by experts, who "methodically take in data, anecdotal cases, and statistics" to form simplified models (Starr and Whipple 1980). While the dimensions of contrast vary slightly in subsequent research, the basic distinction persists (Doderlein 1983; Hohenemser et al. 1983; Kraus et al. 1992; Starr 1985; Wright and Phillips 1986). The so-called intuitive mode of cognition evidenced by nonspecialists has received considerable attention by experimental psychologists. When faced with a complicated decision concerning hazardous occurrences, or one where a great deal of uncertainty is associated with the outcome, the application of commonly used mental short-cuts, or heuristics, often violates statistical principles. In the context of probabilistic risk assessment, a "real" risk is assumed to be embedded in the "true state of nature" (Ozonoff and Boden 1987). It can be calculated, if one acquires a certain technical expertise. The general public, by contrast, is described as distorting the "real" risk with its less analytical approach to risk estimation (Nealey and Radford 1987; Slovic 1987b).

That short-cuts lead to judgments at odds with expected outcomes—as calculated by statistical reasoning—is well documented (see Kahneman and Snell 1992; Kahneman and Tversky 1984; Lopes and Ekberg 1980; Slovic 1987b; Tversky and Kahneman 1974, 1981). The use of various heuristics (for example, "representativeness," "availability," "anchoring," and "framing") are said to inaccurately estimate both the probability of occurrences and the magnitude of their consequences. If laypersons generally do not form risk judgments solely on the basis of statistical reasoning, however, does this necessarily require that they be excluded from risk-management decisions? Moreover, if violating principles of statistical reasoning is an exclusionary criterion, what are we to do with the experts, whose judgments of risk have also been shown to depart from these principles? The distinction between "risk" and "uncertainty" is important here (see Douglas 1985:43). When we are concerned with known probabilities of alternative outcomes, conditions of "risk" obtain. We are operating under conditions of "uncertainty," however, when the range of alternative outcomes, as well as their likelihood of occurrence, may not be known. Reliance on statistical reasoning under conditions of uncertainty lends a false precision to specialists' judgments. As Hammond et al. point out:

> When citizens and their representatives demand to know "How much risk does a given installation or action impose on the population likely to be affected?" scientists and engineers can seldom immediately perform the experiments, or carry out the statistical studies, that will provide rigorously derived answers. Rather, they must almost invariably extrapolate and generalize from the pure science of the laboratory to circumstances not yet studied. To do so, they must resort to "judgment." Without the cognitive safeguards provided by the fully analytical methods of logic and experimentation, scientists who exercise judgment are reduced to employing the same quasi-rational cognitive processes that laypersons must use, with much the same consequences, uncertainty, misunderstanding, and persistent dispute. [1984:69–70]

Beyond framing problems in statistics, judgment is also required in deciding how best to provide information for citizens and policy makers. In this undertaking, judgment must be used to:

- Determine the presumed level of technical sophistication of the intended audience
- Evaluate the intended audience's tolerance for inconclusiveness
- Decide how much of the inevitable internal technical disagreements are to be revealed publicly
- Determine a suitable time for making such information available

An Alternative View of Nonspecialists

Although beyond debate among most ethnographers, I often find myself having to argue to policy makers that nonspecialists do have expertise to offer, based on strategically instituted responses they have made to "subcritical" events. Their collective judgments about technology-related environmental risks should be given greater credence, and strategies for accommodating such risks should be modified accordingly.

Olson (1987) distinguishes three types of recurring events: everyday events, exceptional events, and those lying between the extremes. Everyday events, of course, are widely observed, measured, labeled, discussed, and otherwise given shared meanings. Agricultural producers routinely handle strong chemicals, keep track of their neighbors' production results and correlate these with chemical use, repeat stories about accidents and misuse, and generally agree that the need and benefit of agricultural chemical use outweigh any untoward health and environmental effects that might also result. Exceptional events do not even occur once in a lifetime, but their effects are of extreme magnitude. Because they recur so infrequently, however, the calculus used to gauge their effects may be outmoded by the next occurrence. Comparing these effects over such a lapse of time is all but impossible, with the full meaning of the earlier experience often imperfectly conveyed to latter day citizens. Neighbors of the proposed incinerator site can recall the spectacular eruption of Mount St. Helens in 1980, befouling farming equipment and ruining the spring planting season. And even though it didn't affect them nearly so directly, they also recall as extraordinary the death of a prized Japanese race horse in 1986. Its owners suspected tainted feed flown in especially from Kansas as the cause of death. Specialty hay growers in Kansas were all but eliminated from the export market for several years.

In-between, or subcritical, events are possibly of greatest relevance here; they are events recalled from the past and expected in the future. Because they are likely to occur at least once within one's lifetime, a model of interpretation is required, and cultural practices must ensure that experience of the older generation will be brought to bear when the event recurs. The human response to occasional hazards depends on subcritical events considered to be of the same type. Already noted is the notion of "signal" effects inherent in certain technologies—those located at a particular intersection of "dread" and "unknown" in their psychometric factor space (Fischhoff et al. 1981; Slovic 1987a). Even minor departures from normal in the operation of these technologies are taken as "signals" that a potentially greater hazard awaits. Among the collective effects of these subcritical events are the maintenance of community recall and refinement of a calculus for gauging their implications. Thus a local model is developed and reinforced, calling attention to the potentially hazardous consequences not only for the infrequent events of lesser magnitude, but also the exceptional event. Expectations of subcritical events are modified by experience. A discount rate is applied (defining roughly the horizon beyond which events become largely irrelevant to the decision). The event remote in the past is perceived as remote or unlikely in the near future. Although a dramatic environmental crisis recedes historically, it can be revived by an event of magnitude. Thus a collective model is developed for exploring the environment and for searching our social experience for strategies of response. Such strategies are continually subjected to testing.

The point is that problems of forecasting and contingency planning can occupy as large a place in the popular domain as they do in more specialized domains of knowledge. Rarely do specific development proposals involving dangerous or uncertain technologies come out of the blue, the result of an unprecedented encounter with affected communities.

To illustrate how these in-between events might prompt the development of a response strategy, it is instructive to examine the historical context that frames the interactions between the U.S. Department of Energy and Indian tribes of the Pacific Northwest. Conflicting views of the federal government as an agent of both prosperity and devastation have developed over long-standing, repeated exposure that people in the surrounding communities have had to:

- Ravaging disease (in the lifetimes of Indian people who were personally known to people alive today)
- Loss of land base and traditional subsistence resources over a period of less than a generation (in the lifetimes of Indian people who were personally known to people alive today)
- Near-total destruction of the Columbia River anadromous fishery by converting this enormous river into a chain of languishing reservoirs (in the lifetimes of both Indian and non-Indian people alive today)
- Removal from native communities of whole cohorts of children, sent to boarding schools where strong sanctions were leveled against speaking one's native language or visiting home (in the lifetimes of Indian people alive today)
- Revelations that unannounced accidental, routine, and experimental releases of ionizing radiation may have exposed perhaps thousands of workers and nearby residents to contamination (in the lifetimes of people alive today)
- Major fluctuations in local employment and income, due to national policy shifts (in the lifetimes of people alive today)

In each of these instances, even more exceptional consequences were probably averted. However, in each case, accompanying the trauma and visible signs of destruction were assurances from federal agents to the effect of either "it's for your own good" or "a higher national purpose is being served." Far from reassuring, such statements have served only to engender mistrust; they resonate with inequity and cast doubt on the technical expertise of those who discount (or fail to acknowledge) the dire consequences of federal actions. They are offered to deflect responsibility, and in some instances such statements have been misleading, if not patently inaccurate.

Advice to Ethnographers: Get "Inside" the Decision-Making Process

To this point I have suggested that choices available to reduce environmental hazards will be structured differently, depending on the sorts of cultural knowledge that are introduced to the decision-making process. I have also argued that upon further examination, it becomes more difficult to distinguish between "experts" and "laypersons" on the basis of "facts" or "values" informing their risk-related judgments. What I want to suggest now is that the privileged position of "facts" in decision making also privileges the fact-bearers' "values," that this is problematic in a pluralistic democracy, and that the privileging of fact-bearers' values over those of laypersons is not necessarily apparent from "outside" the process by which public-policy decisions are made. This perspective is offered to further encourage ethnographers to get "inside" the decision-making process, since from there it is possible both to (1) locate applicable cultural knowledge and, equally important, as Cerroni-Long suggests, (2) retrieve this knowledge in a form the decision-making process recognizes as authoritative.

In the two decades since Laura Nader gave us the term "studying up," I think the topography of decision-making power has changed very little. Despite modest fiddling with the timing and nature of public involvement in public agency decision making, a great chasm still exists between policy makers and the public(s) whose interests they purport to serve. However, an ample cohort of ethnographers has made its way "up"—not just actuarially, but institutionally as well—and obstacles that once loomed large are now considerably less formidable. One will recall Nader's appeal for a more urgent anthropology:

> [T]he quality of life and our lives themselves may depend upon the extent to which citizens understand those who shape attitudes and actually control institutional structures. The study of man is confronted with an unprecedented situation: never before have so few, by their actions and inactions, had the power of life and death over so many members of the species. [1974:284]

The obstacles she acknowledged were problems of access, an endemic professional preference to root for the underdog, ethical confusions derived from gaining private confidences from public servants, and having few other methods to draw from our tool kits when office workers don't want to cooperate with the project of participant-observation.

Lack of Access as an Obstacle

Access to decision makers, it strikes me, is not nearly as overpowering an obstacle as it once might have been to ethnographers. Despite a general orientation of resistance (or denial) whose origins come from an earlier formative period, many professional ethnographers today occupy secure, responsible positions in large, hierarchical institutions. In these positions, many ethnographers spend a good deal of time meeting in small groups making decisions—formulating recommendations, articulating strategic planning goals and objectives, allocating financial scarcities—or talking individually with colleagues, allies (prospective, current, or former), or ancient and honorable gatekeepers, to anticipate or rehash these same decisions. In addition, many professional ethnographers attend scrupulously to cultivating and maintaining personal network ties that extend a span of information sources for possible application to both scholarly and administrative pursuits. When one stops and thinks just a bit, these same network ties can be (and often are) mobilized to gain access to counterparts in other kinds of institutions, where we are well prepared to honor the local artifacts, architecture, and activity patterns that animate such institutions.

How does having such access help one locate applicable cultural knowledge? First, there is a matter of logistics. Entrance to controlled buildings and direct personal correspondence via telephone, fax, and electronic mail afford the participant-observer a close-in vantage point from which to view the ongoing stream of agency events. In turn, this perspective helps to produce an understanding of formally and informally instituted normative patterns and procedures within the agency's central office, including the agency staffers' view of the agency's mission and of the agency's preferred resolution to major conflicts that may surface with groups outside the agency.

A Preference for the Underdog

Once upon a time we took great delight in pointing out how cultural patterns that appear counterintuitive or downright other-worldly may indeed be quite reasonable, given the local circumstances that give rise to them. This should hold equally true for those who pull the purse and power strings as it does for peasants and artisanal fishers. But it doesn't. For an ethnographer, becoming closely enough affiliated with decision-makers to make sense of their circumstances inevitably distances one from the decision-makers' constituents. On the other hand, the ethnographer who believes she or he remains untainted, identifying most closely with a particular community, may have such a polarized view of how public policy decisions are made that she or he is unable to retrieve locally held knowledge in a form the decision-making process recognizes as authoritative. In thinking more carefully of who is the underdog (and whose viewpoint is privileged in a conflict over environmental risk), it may be of value to recall Levine and Campbell's (1984) discussion of the problem of group boundaries in recognizing the innocuous source of much of this polarization. Levine and Campbell point out that too often, ethnographers assume, rather than leaving as an open question, that a group is a group is a group. If it has a name, frequently the "group" is presumed to represent discontinuities in language, economy, sociopolitical structure, and ideology. In a unit so distinguished from its neighbors, each institutionalized aspect of social action has the properties of an organized entity, with interdependent parts and a normally high degree of stability (Levine and Campbell 1984:83). Such a clearly identified group, it can be argued, is the exception, not the rule. Especially when the presumed culture-bearing unit is a formal organization (like a public agency), assuming that it is well bounded may lead us to neglect the intercultural context of social action and to falsely secure conclusions about social and cultural processes. For example, if one assumes that a policy agency is a coherent unit, initial perceptions in the field are likely to be structured accordingly. We will seek named territorial units and discontinuities associated with their boundaries. Once units have been identified, they will be used to set limits on the extent of investigations, overlooking continuities and interdependencies across the boundaries. As the fieldwork so initiated progresses, the data themselves tend to convince the ethnographer that she or he is dealing with a sharply bounded entity constituting a functioning system; she or he may not recognize that it has been at least in part a self-fulfilling prophecy. Evidence that casts doubts on standard assumptions concerning groups and their boundaries derives from various factors:

(1) *Territorial interpenetration:* It is not possible to draw a single continuous territorial boundary that separates members of one group from members of another. Just picture the groups supporting or opposing construction of the regional hazardous waste incinerator. Some of the most vocal critics are metropolitan area residents, living hundreds of miles away from the proposed incinerator site. They are concerned about airborne residues contaminating food they buy in grocery stores originating from the site's vicinity. They may also be employed by the industrial firms whose manufacturing activities create the hazardous wastes in need of treatment and disposal. Other critics of the incinerator include the local agriculturalists. They are concerned that the market for their products will be hurt. Yet the land that would be used for the incinerator was originally owned by the rural county government, and sold by this county government to support the company's bid to build the regional incinerator. In addition, the public agency authorized to determine how best to serve the public interest is spatially segmented as well. A decision by the federal government to permit the incinerator's construction is made in stages, first with the regional office of the cognizant agency reviewing the permit application, then passing it along to the national headquarters. A

classic tension is built into the structure of this decision-making process, where the regional office must find a way to accommodate local interests, while the national headquarters is often more concerned with enforcing a rigid consistency among its various regions' permitting decisions.

(2) *Continuous variation in cultural characteristics:* Group boundaries are also made problematic where the distribution of culturally patterned characteristics does not co-vary. This means that if one observer divides a region into communities on the basis of economic or resource-based dissimilarities, another on the basis of native/nonnative distinctions, a third based on legal standing with respect to administrative procedures, and a fourth by named religious affiliations, they will produce different group divisions, each appearing arbitrary and unreal from the viewpoint of the other.

(3) *Disagreement about boundaries or labels:* There is inconsistency among people in their assignment of labels to themselves, and in their use of these labels to mark off one group from another. Where inconsistencies of this sort are pronounced, it is impossible to obtain a set of definitive boundaries based on the conceptions of the people themselves. Multiplicity of group membership is ubiquitous.

(4) *Interaction across group boundaries:* Social groups are rarely social isolates, and group members engage in formal and informal interaction across the boundaries that separate them, especially with the threat of outsiders (e.g., people from the national government or the metropolis).

(5) *Shifts of identity and culturally defined lifestyles:* Individuals and groups change their affiliations on the basis of calculations of strategic advantage. Such change is a recurrent aspect of social process. Visible attributes of cultural difference have become symbols to be manipulated in a struggle for social mobility or political power rather than indications of stable groupings or objects of permanent attachment.

All this is to simply acknowledge that group boundaries are often fluid and problematic, and as ethnographers we generally have some element of choice as to the "group" with which we identify as "insiders." In conflict situations, we often assume inappropriately the salience of group boundaries (whether these groups are "risk experts" or populations at risk, for example), which leads, in turn, to a reification of the groups' status and coherence, and a polarization where joint-problem solving is sought.

Methods and Ethics

Ethnographic work "inside" the decision-making process presents methodological and ethical challenges for which no simple prescription is available. Participant-observation methods can be seen as intrusive—especially when the very question at issue is who qualifies to be part of a more or less selective decision-making group. Less obtrusive methods lose the richness of detail that direct observation yields, and a central analytical problem that would go undetected by relying on secondary sources and reconstructed accounts concerns the relationship a documented record of decision making actually bears to the way in which the decision was reached. Construction of such records is shaped by individuals' intentions and by patterned organizational practices worth examining.

Such an examination is only possible, however, with corroborating observations from someone less vested in the outcome, that is, the ethnographer. Methodologically, the challenge of working up to participant-observer status inside the decision-making process must be accomplished in stages. We constantly work with the following paradox: one's project must make sense to those empowered to grant or deny participant-observation access to the setting, yet the investigation's focus emerges clearly only after some portion of the research has been accomplished.

The paradox is inevitable. The key to resolving it is to employ a progressive strategy in which one gradually increases one's requests for less obtrusive involvement in insider settings. The success of this progressive strategy may depend, in practice, on what Spradley (1980) termed defocusing one's project (providing brief comments to indicate the general substantive interests of the researcher, but leaving the wording as open-ended as possible). Generalized language allows a wider latitude for observing a full range of activities, many of which have yet to be discovered. Also, more general language provides greater freedom to negotiate the purposes of the research at each level of a hierarchical organization.

Ethically, the challenges noted by Laura Nader have not subsided. Observing the exercise of power puts one face to face with authority figures who are likely to be concerned with whether one's ethnographic inquiry may upset plans for policy change; whether information produced will fall into the "wrong" hands, revealing imperfect practices; or possibly even whether such an inquiry will uncover practices of questionable legality. In doing this sort of work, one can expect an early "test" of personal character. One will be asked: "Are you a scientist or an advocate? A spy? What is the true purpose of your work? Do you know what happened to us the last time someone like you was here?" Or even, "What do you think of so-and-so, who has also done work with us?"

As in other ethnographic settings, how one responds to these tests will greatly influence one's subsequent effectiveness as a participant-observer. And things over which one has little control must also be negotiated.

As a consequence of timing, one's appearance on the scene soon after an untoward event (an unfavorable court decision, a reorganization or change of personnel) may raise people's suspicions that one is part of some stepped-up monitoring procedure. Also, it is reasonable to expect that one's arrival and presentation of research plans will bring to the surface divisions within the setting that originate from quite independent sources. Support for one's efforts from some quarters will reflexively result in resistance from others.

Are these obstacles insurmountable? I think not. I think that the practice of anthropology applied specifically to power relations, perhaps more directly than in other domains of application, has had to confront the contested, negotiated nature of "facts" and "values." In the process, we become colleagues of the policy makers; they are not informants, nor are they the "other."

To sum up, then, getting past the disabling effects of an expert/layperson dichotomy helps to locate an enlarged cultural knowledge base relevant to reducing environmental hazards. I also believe that an ethnographic focus on the decision-making process itself can be most productive when it provides a different vantage point from which to make sense of this knowledge base, regarding "fact" and "value" in a complementary rather than hierarchical fashion, and avoiding the trap of privileging either one at the expense of the other.

Notes

This article is based on work conducted under contract with the U.S. Department of Energy, the U.S. Centers for Disease Control and Prevention, and the Environmental Security Corporation. However, the author is solely responsible for the opinions expressed here.

References Cited

Brown, Phil
1987 Popular Epidemiology: Community Response to Toxic Waste-Induced Disease in Woburn, Massachusetts. Science, Technology and Human Values 12(3–4):78–85.
1992 Popular Epidemiology and Toxic Waste Contamination: Lay and Professional Ways of Knowing. Journal of Health and Social Behavior 33:267–281.
Doderlein, Jan M.
1983 Understanding Risk Management. Risk Analysis 3(1):17–21.
Douglas, Mary
1985 Risk Acceptability According to the Social Sciences. Social Research Perspectives. Occasional Reports on Current Topics, 11. New York: Russell Sage Foundation.
1992 Risk and Blame: Essays in Cultural Theory. London: Routledge.
Douglas, Mary, and Aaron Wildavsky
1982 Risk and Culture: An Essay on the Selection of Technological and Environmental Dangers. Berkeley: University of California Press.
Fischhoff, Baruch, Susan Lichtenstein, Paul Slovic, P. Derby, and Ralph Keeney
1981 Acceptable Risk. New York: Cambridge University Press.
Hammond, Kenneth R., Barry F. Anderson, Jeffrey Sutherland, and Barbara Marvin
1984 Improving Scientists' Judgments of Risk. Risk Analysis 4(1):69–78.
Hohenemser, C., R. W. Kates, and P. Slovic
1983 The Nature of Technological Hazard. Science 220:378–384.

Kahneman, Daniel, and Jackie Snell
1992 Predicting A Changing Taste: Do People Know What They Will Like? Journal of Behavioral Decision Making 5:187–200.
Kahneman, Daniel, and Amos Tversky
1984 Choices, Values, and Frames. American Psychologist 39(4):341–350.
Kraus, Nancy, Torbjorn Malmfors, and Paul Slovic
1992 Intuitive Toxicology: Expert and Lay Judgments of Chemical Risks. Risk Analysis 12(2):215–232.
Levine, Robert A., and Donald T. Campbell
1984 Ethnocentrism: Theories of Conflict, Ethnic Attitudes, and Group Behavior. New York: Wiley.
Liebow, Edward B.
1988 Permanent Storage for Nuclear Power Plant Wastes: Comparing Risk Judgments and Their Social Effects. Practicing Anthropology 10(3–4):10–12.
1993 Who Is Expert at Interpreting Environmental Hazards? A Commentary on the Disabling Effects of an Expert/Layperson Dichotomy. Environmental Professional 15(3):288–292.
Liebow, Edward B., Kristi M. Branch, and Carlyn E. Orians
1993 Perceptions of Hazardous Waste Incineration Risks: Focus Group Findings. Sociological Spectrum 13:153–173.
Liebow, Edward B., and Amy K. Wolfe
1993 Communities at Risk: Communication and Choice of Environmental Hazards. Environmental Professional 15(3):237–239.
Lopes, Lola L., and Per-Hakan S. Ekberg
1980 Test of an Ordering Hypothesis in Risky Decision Making. Acta Psychologica 45:161–167.
Nader, Laura
1974 Up the Anthropologist: Perspectives Gained from Studying Up. *In* Reinventing Anthropology. Dell Hymes, ed. Pp. 284–311. New York: Vintage Books.
Nealey, Stanley M., and Linda R. Radford
1987 Public Fear of Nuclear Technology. *In* Waste Management '87: Waste Isolation in the U.S. R. G. Post, ed. Pp. 171–178. Proceedings of the Symposium on Waste Management at Tucson, Arizona, March 1–5. Tucson: University of Arizona Press.
Olson, Sherry
1987 Red Destinies: The Landscape of Environmental Risk in Madagascar. Human Ecology 15(1):67–89.
Ozonoff, David, and Leslie I. Boden
1987 Truth and Consequences: Health Agency Responses to Environmental Health Problems. Science, Technology, and Human Values 12(3–4):70–77.
Rappaport, Roy
1988 Toward Postmodern Risk Analysis. Risk Analysis 8(2):189–191.
Rayner, Steve, and Robin Cantor
1987 How Fair Is Safe Enough? The Cultural Approach to Societal Technological Choice. Risk Analysis 7(1):3–9.
Slovic, Paul
1987a Forecasting the Adverse Economic Effects of a Nuclear Waste Repository. *In* Waste Management '87: Waste Isolation in the U.S. R. G. Post, ed. Pp. 91–94. Proceedings of the Symposium on Waste Management at Tucson, Arizona, March 1–5. Tucson: University of Arizona Press.
1987b Perception of Risk. Science 236:280–285.
Spradley, James P.
1980 Participant Observation. New York: Holt, Rinehart and Winston.
Starr, Chauncey
1985 Risk Management, Assessment, and Acceptability. Risk Analysis 5(2):97–102.
Starr, Chauncey, and Chris Whipple
1980 Risks of Risk Decisions. Science 208:1114–1119.
Tversky, Amos, and Daniel Kahneman
1974 Judgment under Uncertainty: Heuristics and Biases. Science 185:1124–1131.
1981 The Framing of Decisions and the Psychology of Choice. Science 211:453–458.

Wright, George N., and Lawrence D. Phillips
1986 Cultural Variation in Probabilistic Thinking: Alternative Ways of Dealing with Uncertainty. *In* Judgment and Decisionmaking. H. R. Arkes and K. R. Hammond, eds. Pp. 416–431. Cambridge: Cambridge University Press.

The Limits of Detachment: A Non-Ethnography of the Military

Alexandra Jaffe

When I left graduate school in 1983 to serve an obligatory tour in the Army, I shared the assumptions of my colleagues and advisers that this would be a sort of extended period of fieldwork. My first active-duty experience was in a service school, where the social code was exaggerated and artificial even by military standards. This did nothing to dispel the myth to which I had acquiesced in graduate school: that I was a spy in the camp of an ideologically insupportable, lumbering, mindless institution, redeeming my membership somewhat by gathering data.

Four-and-a-half years later, at the end of a tour in Germany, I had come to realize that this academic and conspiratorial view of my military membership was not an honest reflection of my experience in the Army. I did not have a file drawer packed with the dissertation notes I had expected to be ludicrously easy to collect, a matter of coming home at night and jotting it all down. More than a spy, I had begun to feel like a double agent, pulled by two conflicting and competing sets of allegiances. Attempting to reconcile my membership in both the military and academic worlds became a pressing personal concern and led me to reflect on what it was about both military membership and my conception of anthropological practice that made "data collection" so very difficult.

This article is about the tension between the experience of legitimate membership and the practice of ethnography. It is also an exploration of the relationship of this practice to the anthropological discourse, a theme elaborated by Clifford and Marcus (1986), Fernandez (1985), Rabinow (1985), Stoller (1984), and others. There are several thrusts to the current rethinking of ethnography: first of all, the need for "reflexivity" in fieldwork (Babcock 1984; Moore 1978) has brought about acceptance—even a demand—that issues of personal involvement, the "noise in the corridor" (Rabinow 1985) of fieldwork, be incorporated into ethnographic accounts. Along with this call for the expansion of the author's voice has come a revision of notions of ethnographic authority, a concern to incorporate the voices of those being studied into an anthropological dialogue that attempts to evoke an encounter rather than create an authoritative text of an exotic culture. Ultimately, these sets of concerns are political, a fact that is central to the feminist (see di Leonardo 1991; Ortner and Whitehead 1981) and anticolonialist (see Harrison 1991) critiques of anthropology. The ethnographic text is a forum for the negotiation of the power of practice and experience, the many voices of the ethnographic encounter, and the power of the established academic, institutional discourse and its underlying philosophy of knowledge.

My military experience, in which power relations were central, made me particularly sensitive to these issues of authority, realism, observation, and representation in the social sciences. Moreover, being part of the Army forcefully illustrated to me the way the limits of objectivity and detachment are imposed by the day-to-day enactment of membership. Both the social ideology and the individual experience of identity (especially in societies where individualism is highly valued) makes the relationship between the essence and the social expression of self look necessary, absolute, and referential. The naturalization of identity through culture denies the contingent, relative, and metaphorical nature of meaning, and enables the legitimacy of Being to be an unquestioned point of departure for "abstract" operations of reflection and analysis.

But my experience as an anthropologist in the Army also emphasizes to me that the dynamics of involvement/detachment are extremely complex and are influenced by factors that the ethnographer can only partly control. Was it impossible for me, or any other Army officer, to write an ethnography of the military? No. I could have, if I had chosen to resist my desire to adapt and belong, if I had hated my jobs, if I had been stuck on a God-forsaken post with nothing to do (as it was, I was stationed near Heidelberg), if I had worked shorter hours, if I had gone into the Army completely and sincerely convinced that it was only relevant as a field experience from which a dissertation had to be produced. The extent to which some of these factors influenced me is idiosyncratic, but I believe that considerations of this kind have an enormous, and often unpredictable, effect on the practice of ethnography in general. The point is that ethnography is not about resolving, but exploring the relationship between involvement and detachment that is part of life in general. Reflexivity or involvement cannot be turned on or off at the will of the ethnographer, who carries an extensive baggage of social/personal history and academic assumptions into the field. While it may be desirable to unpack these tacit assumptions, it is often very difficult and sometimes disquieting.

Thus, going from the academic to the military world, I expected the novelty of the ritualization and hierarchy of the Army to facilitate ethnographic observation. I assumed that my military identity would remain secondary and that my concerns as an officer would never seem as real and legitimate as carrying out my academic training. At the heart of my assumptions about military duty was a belief that the ideology of membership, and the values and value of the institution in the abstract, had a primary, determinate effect on the experience of membership. I did not believe that the ethical/ideological premises of military membership were as inherently valuable as those of the academic world. Because of my fundamental pessimism about human nature I accepted the existence of the military, and I believed I could act morally in a morally neutral but potentially ill-used organization. Given my position of guarded neutrality on the morality of military participation, I expected my sense of belonging to be equally guarded and lukewarm.

The most interesting and, in some ways, most frustrating aspect of my short military career was my unexpected level of involvement. The fact that I did not expect to become absorbed in military life stemmed in part from my previous, nonreflective immersion in the academic social structure and ideology, from which I inherited some negative attitudes about hierarchy (epitomized by military social organization) and the military ideology: the Army was the sort of organization in which other people became involved. The unexpectedness also derived from the view, shared and reinforced by both my academic and military associates, that these two worlds were completely different domains of practice and ideology; I was treated as a curiosity in both.

The most significant social contrast is in the structures and the value of control. In the academic world, these structures are backgrounded: the organization is supposed to exist in order to facilitate individual intellectual achievement. On the contrary, social controls are central to both the ideology and the operation of the military, in which the individual exists for the organization, which exists as a means towards a limited set of national, political ends. Since the military views the great mass of its members as potentially, but not inherently or consistently, able or responsible, the reach of its social regulations extends into almost every realm of the professional and personal lives of its members. At the university the structures of social control are not only fewer and less overt, they are also framed as external, administrative, and secondary, less worthy than the academic domain.

Thus I thought of my entry into the Army as a new type, rather than as a variation of familiar experience. Despite the fact that I had left the university as a doctoral candidate, the relative lack of overt, doctrinal socialization in the academic practice had desensitized me to the powerful influences and demands of the society and encouraged a self-gratifying confidence in the autonomous, rational nature of my membership. I did not recognize the university as a total institution (in Goffman's [1961] sense of the term), different in style, rather than form, from the military. I expected to have to battle the logic of military membership in order to maintain a sense of self.

The extent to which both the military and academic environments are total institutions that structure a vast amount of individual experience reinforced my perception that they were mutually exclusive communities of practice and value. Neither group views the other as inherently valuable, therefore the peculiarities of its mechanisms of social control, stratification, dress, customs, and language seem arbitrary and ridiculous. The philosophical polarization of the military and the university makes difference necessary; no matter how much bureaucracies look alike, their members create chasms of differentiation, on principle, out of the finest detail.

All my fellow officers were college graduates, and some of my fellow students had been in the military. But in each case there was a clear sense of transition, of passage and progress. Because switching from one social domain to the other demanded a large emotional and social investment in a new role, the world left behind looked bizarre and unreal in retrospect. A lot of officers did sweat through years of extension night courses for a "career advancing" M.A. in fields with a direct application to their military occupations. Full-time studenthood was a remembered luxury of youth, a time of comparatively little responsibility. Those with a strong academic background found it of little practical use or consequence to their social standing. In fact, social display of more than the required or instrumental amount of education was viewed with suspicion, and men (much more than women, who were exempt from most of the "macho" standards of military evaluation) were judged in spite of their intellectual achievements, as if being an academic precluded being a tough or efficient soldier. The Army was the world of real work, the university of either play or drudgery, depending on the individual's perspective.

Other graduate students who had been in the Army had been recruited to serve in Vietnam, whose shadow of horror and immorality unalterably and understandably colored their perception of the military. Their reflections on military social organization all centered around the oppression of hierarchy and the absurdity of military bureaucracy, which had hit them at full force as members of the lower ranks. They talked about the military in terms of its structural properties, as an artifact, thus keeping at a distance the traumatic nature of their experience. In general, the rest of the university community was even more predisposed than the veterans to distrust or despise the function of the wartime military and the social structure of the peacetime Army.

My strong sense of contrast between my military and academic identities and experiences was based on both my own a priori philosophical assumptions about the relative values of the two institutions, and the very real differences in their style of social life. Coupled with the polarized view of military and academic life held by those around me, both my theories and the reality of difference led me to view my two lives as mutually exclusive and untranslatable.

I did not expect to pursue a policy of detachment from military service, but I did look forward to a continuing novelty of participation in a rigid, explicitly hierarchical organization. But the novelty wore off, faster than I ever imagined. I was caught up, unaware, in the uniquely compelling nature of the style of military life and felt a commitment that was ill suited to my academic self-image. This was yet another psychological incentive to segregate and compartmentalize my military from my academic self and, in effect, cut the ethnographic role out of my everyday existence.

To redeem my (now primary) role as an anthropologist, I will try to describe what it is about the military that binds individual to role so effectively.

The mechanisms of this process are unremarkable and common, I think, to the workings of most institutions. But the Army does distinguish itself by a heavy-handedness, a clumsy, unapologetic, and surprisingly efficient acknowledgment of its intentions in the manipulation of symbols, practices, and forms of control.

One of the first lessons of military training has to do with the display of ideology, the performance of commitment. The military establishment understands that the conditions of military membership challenge common American social conceptions of egalitarianism and individualism. Consequently, the military demands a display of ideological commitment from its members at almost every juncture of military life, and incorporates symbolic display into internal customs and organization as well as in the rules for the "presentation of self" to the outside, civilian world. The wearing of uniforms and haircut regulations are good examples of the imposition of ideologically laden systems of self-presentation. Within the organization, adherence to the minimum standards is a required expression of individual compliance. Consistently challenging social tolerance of minor or temporary lapses (by getting a haircut only when the hair has been too long for weeks, or by keeping a moustache that is slightly but not excessively over the allowed width) is interpreted as a "bad attitude" toward the system as a whole. Zealous attention to military appearance, maintaining stricter standards than required, is taken as evidence of commitment and belief in the system.

The body of the individual soldier is viewed as a microcosm of the body politic and its demands for discipline and uniformity. The collective appearance of military personnel is also explicitly defined as a demonstration of pride of membership and solidarity to the civilian world. In some places, concern with the image of the organization has led commanders to forbid the wearing of fatigue (work) uniforms in public places around the installation.

Wearing a uniform or having a military haircut outside the military environment also serves to impress the wearer with the social ramifications of membership, whether they are positive or negative. I still remember my intense self-consciousness during the semester I was unable to change out of my ROTC uniform before a class in 17th-century poetry. This hazard of scheduling made my (then partial) commitment to the military public and forced me to consider my choice in the light of the possible ideological objections I projected onto my academic audience; an audience to which I belonged, out of uniform. These kinds of sentiments, I am sure, are shared by basic trainees, heads shorn, on their first trip into town as soldiers.

In time I viewed my uniform as a natural extension of a multifaceted military identity with which I had some depth of experience, rather than as an outfit that stood for a role with one dimension: its difference from the civilian world. The next time I felt disconcerted by being in uniform was while I was "out-processing" from the Army. I felt like a caricature: I looked and felt a part that I could not felicitously display or express to those who were shuffling me through the administrative process. My uniform was a sign of a relationship of loyalty to the system that was the heart of my identity as an officer, an identity I was resigning. The routine, almost subconscious expectations I had built up over several years about social encounters with other military people began to dissolve. They had all been based on rank. I was no longer certain of, or comfortable with, the attitudes I attributed to the military people I encountered who knew I was "getting out." Some of the enlisted clerks presumed a fellowship of disaffection with the system, leveling the difference of rank. Others, officers and enlisted, treated me with the inscrutable courtesy of strangers, which stripped all the external signs of common membership (linguistic courtesies, uniform insignia, salutes) of meaning. During this terminal period I still viewed my departure from within.

I mention this experience in order to emphasize that the nature of my involvement in the military had a great deal to do with being an officer. Differences in the socialization of officers and enlisted men illustrate that the organization expects junior officers to buy into the system, but it considers the first term of enlistment a trial period in which both the organization and the individual reserve the right of detachment and entertain, but do not promise, the possibility of involvement.

The focus of the numerous sociological analyses of basic training is always motivated by a fascination with a rite of passage, perhaps because ours is a society that has relatively few. Much has been written about the psychological effect of having all the outward expressions of individuality stripped away to be replaced with the emblems and logic of an institutional identity. Basic training is about power, but the hyper-ritualization of the military socialization process is less about belief in the new role than it is about the display of belief in the enactment of the basic rules. The training process imposes a new, albeit restricted, idiom of self-expression in which the foregrounded message is commitment and belief in the justice and integrity of the system. However, the very rigidity of the form of this message allows the perceptive and disaffected recruit to "fake it," to survive with a distant and uncommitted compliance.

This strategy is tacitly condoned (although not rewarded) for low-ranking enlisted people, whose stake in the system is small and whose privileges are few. In fact, very minimal compliance with haircut standards is a common, collective emblem of the lower enlisted community, who often openly express their dislike for military life. However, this sort of behavior completely violates the standards of behavior for officers. Thus I found that I had entered a social stratum in which my identity, belief, and performance were expected to be congruent.

At a very basic level, my behavior was assumed to reflect a belief in the value of military membership and a commitment to represent the system. The cumulative effect of my enactment of military rule and custom was far more powerful than any of my military training, from which I was suitably detached. In almost every sphere of military life I was obliged to play by rules and customs that were patently, unabashedly arbitrary and therefore inherently valueless. It was the putting into practice that acquired value; in fact, the performance of arbitrary rules only served to emphasize the central fact of my military life as an officer: I was the system; I embodied and enacted it. Half-hearted membership is psychologically unpalatable in this sort of system; if I was to accept the sometimes ridiculous demands of everyday military life—and I had to—the only way to exempt myself from the ridiculous without maintaining a constant distance from my role was to legitimize the value of the organization in general, and therefore my part in it.

The case of rank is a good example. Despite the evidence of undeserved promotions, despite the fact that the passage from second to first lieutenant and from first lieutenant to captain has a 95 percent success rate, the privileges and obligations of rank pervade so much of military life that it is impossible to experience rank as meaningless. The social and professional impact of the promotion to captain—which is the first officer rank accorded any automatic credibility or authority—is so striking that it inspires belief in the system: other promotions may have no meaning, but in one's own case the system can be congratulated for achieving a perfect fit of person and status.

What is most important is that in every military situation, and at every juncture in a military career, the officer is forced to justify his or her identity, to take a moral stance toward the system, to correct and take responsibility for the behavior and "attitudes" of subordinates, to administer military justice, swear oaths, to be "on duty" 24 hours a day: to represent the system or leave it. So, for four years, I represented it. I became attached to the military rituals of identity, was annoyed to see a soldier with hair that was too long, bristled at a forgotten or ignored salute. For two years I was one of two women army captains on a huge Air Force base in Germany, and was one of two women officers in a NATO-wide project group composed of senior, male, European officers. Being so often in several minorities only added weight to the representative nature of my military role.

In short, I bought in, and lost the desire to be primarily an observer of my own life. I could not, of course, shed my training as an anthropologist any more than I could remove or forget the rank sewn to my uniform collar. But it was a deliberate, conscious, and difficult effort to step outside in order to look in. This is in part because describing and classifying social action gives it a fixity that runs counter to nonreflexive everyday experience. The fruitfulness of the ethnographic encounter, traditionally with exotic cultures, comes from a sense of contrast between systems of meaning and value. As Crapanzano points out (1986), ethnographies must first convey the strangeness and apparent meaninglessness of a foreign culture before transforming it into something intelligible with analysis. My discomfort with using my military life as ethnographic data had to do, in part, with the necessity of keeping that sense of strangeness at the surface of experience when, in fact, most of my everyday life contradicted this theoretical apprehension of the forms of military society.

In a sense, I see my experience of the military, my resistance to a systematic interrogation of the fundamental conditions of my own existence, as a temporary refuge from the inherent tensions of observation, participation, and description that I have sought out on other occasions, in travel, and in anthropology. As a solitary traveler I have enjoyed the bittersweet, liminal status of the observer, enjoying the ability to sample food, scenery, and atmosphere selectively, without the burden of full membership. Like Walter Mitty I could enjoy my secret life as a scholar (and now my submerged military persona) as a means of temporary and private escape, without sacrificing the benefits of socially sanctioned full membership. This sort of detachment, like anthropological practice, must be seen as a social strategy in the continuous negotiation of identity: the public or private declaration of distance is an act of individual power. At the same time, this sort of declaration can undermine the equally compelling and necessary faith in the social contract by exposing the individual to the uncontrollable effects of the freedom of others. There is no such thing as pure involvement, and pure reflexivity is schizophrenic: a constant interruption of the activity of Being in which the individual is hard at work trying to anchor fragmented, multilayered, and loosely interwoven senses of identity in the mundane, uncontemplative, and socially legitimate practice of everyday life.

In the early stages of my tour I looked at my military role in the narrowest sense of the dramaturgical model: as a marked, highly regulated, front-region activity with little room for individual expression and, therefore, little demand for emotional investment. The fact that I become involved is an index of the affective power of the enactment of socially managed public display. The overt controls of performance in the military had the opposite effect from what I expected; the constant demand for consistent performance of the values of the organizational structure made it impossible for me to experience my self and my military self as separate without constructing (and constantly reconstructing) my life as a farce. I was unable to devalue my initial choice of military service by performing insincerely, by maintaining a constant distance between identity and role.

It was also significant that the social enactment of military roles symbolized, expressed, and embodied the very core of military existence and belief: the social hierarchy. I didn't just play at being a lieutenant or a captain—I believed I should be treated in accordance with my rank; I acted up to and out from the structural limitations and potential of my position. While I was involved in the experience of the military structure in practical, political and ideological terms, I resisted an anthropological interpretation of the forms of military life that would only serve to throw into relief the contingency of the relationship between form and meaning. As Bourdieu (1977, 1990) and Gellner (1974) have pointed out, the legitimation of experience demands that arbitrary interpretive or conceptual models be made (or made to look) necessary.

I was able to study the salute. The topic suggested itself because of the extent to which military people discuss saluting, which they explicitly interpret as a gloss on the nature of the organization, the social distribution of power, and the character of individual involvement. It was not disconcerting to attempt to catalog and analyze a gesture that had certainly become habitual and instinctive to me. Nor did I cease to be involved in the act of saluting in an ordinary way; the act of observation and analysis did not trivialize the experience. I think that this was in part because describing salutes from an anthropological perspective is consistent with the experience of saluting: it is the use of one metalanguage to describe another. But the fact that I placed such great value on this consistency also serves to illustrate that I had overstepped the boundaries of the liminality that is the key to ethnography: I was too much a member. I resisted the textualization of much of the uncritical, nonreflective aspects of my military life because I feared the "colonization," and its implication of relations of unequal power, of my military experience by an academic discourse. Having set up and lived a rigid academic/military dichotomy of ideology and practice, I found it difficult to believe that one domain of discourse could accurately or fairly represent the other. I use the word *represent* deliberately, for I was not thinking in metaphorical or allegorical terms and had what I now consider an unfounded doubt about the possibility or value of an anthropological discourse about the meeting of these two cultures.

I became progressively less interested in describing or analyzing the "tacit knowledge" underlying military ritual, custom, and organization. To concentrate on the subject matter of classic ethnographic chapter headings seemed trite and, like the production of "native" performances for tourist consumption, a way of trivializing the key issues of military membership to which I was particularly sensitive: the experience of military identity and power, individual accommodation and interpretation of unique aspects of military organization. Being on the inside, I was interested in eliciting opinions, interpretations, and understandings about military life on the same level of intimacy as I experienced it.

In retrospect, this seems like a somewhat biased concept of ethnography. However, it was true that although I could participate, observe, and engage in all kinds of informal conversations in which rank was relatively unimportant, I could not systematically ask basic, "outsider" questions of a large (that is, outside my normal reach) sample of the military population without compromising the legitimacy of my insider status. I could not spend the bulk of my time asking questions unrelated to my job without risking the perception that I did not take my work seriously. Very often it is the process of apprenticeship that builds intimacy between ethnographers and those they study (see Rapp 1986). Intimacy among insiders, on the other hand, is built on mutual knowledge and shared, tacit assumptions. Questioning cannot be neutral, since it is always colored by relationships of relative rank. My position carried built-in limitations on the kinds of information I could exchange or request from others, based on their rank. For example, I did not have the right to ask personal questions of my superiors; I could ask these questions of a subordinate, but not without arousing suspicion about my possible official motives for prying.

My failure to be a consistent and dedicated observer of military life has been a useful ethnographic and ethnological experience. My experience of the complacent blindness, the uncritical acceptance of membership, was foregrounded in the military, where the formal impetus for involvement was stronger than in many ethnographic encounters. Yet it taught me not to underestimate the power and unpredictability of involvement and detachment in any fieldwork situation, where the ethnographer is pushed and pulled by immediate and distant social and professional influences. The parameters of my military role were clearly bounded; the role of the ethnographer is usually more open-ended. However, in the practice of ethnography, people are in the business of constructing a persona that they can live with and through, both as temporary members of a society in which they do not have primary social status, and as members of a community of anthropologists with professional and intellectual beliefs and responsibilities. Some of the constraints on this performance are imposed from without and are experienced as pragmatic demands that have little to do with internal states. But doing fieldwork also involves an active performance of faith in the validity of ethnography, which is the groundwork for the sincere apprehension of individual identity. The construction and enactment of the anthropologist's field role and identity is critical to the way data are conceptualized and collected; yet this social persona usually evolves far from the critical eyes of academic colleagues, often to be shed on return, never to be discussed. In effect, the ethnographer leads two legitimate lives that only rarely touch in the ethnography, although they are practically inseparable. The false sense of untranslatability that I felt in the Army keeps them apart.

So I am skeptical of accounts that excise the personal from the ethnographic dimension, especially insofar as the conflicting pushes and pulls of membership are concerned. But I do not wish to suggest that ethnography should be a form of personal confession. Recognizing the shifting degrees of involvement in fieldwork is only ethnographically significant in a comparative framework, as part of a general philosophy of knowledge. Ethnography is a discourse of identity that takes place on several levels: personal, social, historical, intellectual. This discourse of differentiation (see Elias 1987; Fabian 1983; Herzfeld 1987) is a process of discovery that is always moral and political (that is, relative and contingent) and commonly perceived as neither. Looking at knowledge and identity as context dependent disturbs a rational, voluntaristic view of academic practice and progress. Despite the fact that the academic hierarchy exerts as many social and ideological pressures on individual experience as the far more explicit workings of the military, it is part of the ethos of the academic organization to place as little emphasis as possible on its own political structure and nature. So a good deal of the academic craft—the production and maintenance of authoritative discourses—is shuffled into the background. "Going to the field" can be a mystified activity. To unpack and dissect the process of fieldwork undermines its unquestioned value.

Turning to the relationship of ethnographer to the academic society, it is clear that the cultural relativism that is bound up with doing fieldwork is very relative, and that doing fieldwork does not force the ethnographer to examine or question the basic structures of academic faith and power. Strange local practices may challenge ethnographers' preconceptions on a personal level they need not see as sociologically significant, or draw their attention to broad cultural contrasts that may not penetrate their conception of their own profession and its practices. The experience of fieldwork would be trivialized if, the entire time, the anthropologist thought only of the academic hierarchy, of chances of promotion and publication, of the constraints of the accepted descriptive and analytical discourse. But it is a mistake to view this discourse and hierarchy as I saw military structure, as an imposed and resisted obstacle to individual expression; the system is also a moral and practical universe of belief. Some fieldwork experiences do not fit the academic mold, but just as many are filtered, selected, and experienced in terms of basic theoretical tenets. That the act of perception is theoretical and moral is a commonplace, but to recognize this makes it no easier to disentangle life and belief.

Despite the fact that a demand for a reflexive rendering of the fieldwork experience has chipped away at the status of the third-person, aloof model of ethnographic description, it has not eliminated the need for an authoritative voice. The challenge is to not only recognize the inevitability of the politicization and sanctification of knowledge and practice, but also to come to grips with the shifting limits of involvement and detachment which affect observation, description, and analysis. It is the delicate balance between involvement and detachment, metaphor and literality, in both the practice of fieldwork and its textualization, that should be the aim of anthropology. Clifford (1986) characterizes ethnography as an allegorical practice. I would add that it is an allegory and a practice that its writers can never completely control.

References Cited

Babcock, Barbara
1984 Reflexivity: Definitions and Discriminations. Semiotica 30:1–14.
Bourdieu, Pierre
1977 Outline of a Theory of Practice. Cambridge: Cambridge University Press.
1990 In Other Words. Stanford, CA: Stanford University Press.

Clifford, James
1986 On Ethnographic Allegory. *In* Writing Culture. James Clifford and George E. Marcus, eds. Pp. 98–122. Berkeley: University of California Press.
Clifford, James, and George E. Marcus, eds.
1986 Writing Culture. Berkeley: University of California Press.
Crapanzano, Vincent
1986 Hermes' Dilemma: The Masking of Subversion in Ethnographic Description. *In* Writing Culture. James Clifford and George E. Marcus, eds. Pp. 51–77. Berkeley: University of California Press.
di Leonardo, Micaela, ed.
1991 Gender at the Crossroads of Knowledge. Berkeley: University of California Press.
Elias, Norbert
1987 Involvement and Detachment. New York: Basil Blackwell.
Fabian, Johannes
1983 Time and the Other: How Anthropology Makes Its Object. New York: Columbia University Press.
Fernandez, James
1985 Exploded Worlds: Text as Metaphor for Ethnography. Dialectical Anthropology 10(1/2):15–26.
Gellner, Ernest
1974 The Legitimation of Belief. New York: Cambridge University Press.
Goffman, Erving
1961 Asylums. Chicago: Aldine Publishing Company.
Harrison, Faye, ed.
1991 Decolonizing Anthropology. Washington, DC: American Anthropological Association.
Herzfeld, Michael
1987 Anthropology through the Looking Glass. New York: Cambridge University Press.
Moore, Sally Falk
1978 Law as Process. Boston: Routledge and Kegan Paul.
Ortner, Sherry, and Harriet Whitehead, eds.
1981 Sexual Meanings. New York: Cambridge University Press.
Rabinow, Paul
1985 Discourse and Power: On the Limits of Ethnographic Texts. Dialectical Anthropology 10(1/2):1–15.
Rapp, Rayna
1986 Ritual of Reversion: On Fieldwork and Festivity in Haute Provence. Critique of Anthropology 6(2):35–48.
Stoller, Paul
1984 Eye, Mind and Word in Anthropology. L'Homme 24(3/4):91–114.

Studying Up and the Issue of Cultural Relativism

Mari Womack

Laura Nader's challenge (1974) to anthropologists to "study up"—to study the centers of power—has become even more relevant as anthropologists increasingly conduct research in their own societies. But studying up calls for a searching examination of the assumptions underlying anthropology. Nader asks: "Is there one ethic for studying up and another for studying down?" (1974:304). This question has much to do with the issue of cultural relativism.

In studying traditional societies, anthropologists have advocated the principle of cultural relativism, which has been widely interpreted as adopting a nonjudgmental framework toward the people being studied. This has been especially useful in providing insight into cultural practices that may be incomprehensible unless researchers shed their traditional assumptions about the nature of the world. In studying one's own society, and especially in studying up, does that approach still hold?

Implicit in the principle of cultural relativism is that anthropologists have traditionally studied people who are often powerless in the face of change that threatens to engulf them. Typically, the culture of the people being studied is threatened by the same society represented by the anthropologists studying them and for whom the anthropologists are preparing their ethnographies. Though anthropologists often come to identify with the people they study, the harsh reality is that anthropologists are traditionally members of the colonizing culture and are in the position of interpreting the colonized culture for the colonizer. This is the context in which Franz Boas asserted that the idea of a "cultured" individual is merely relative (1901).

Anthropologists, by virtue of their positions as outsiders, are more powerful than the people they study. When conducting research in complex societies, anthropologists often choose to do research among the poor and disenfranchised, so they retain their position of power vis-à-vis the people they study. There are many reasons for studying down, as Nader puts it. She notes that it is easier to gain access to people who are powerless; in addition, anthropologists have traditionally taken a romantic view of the poor and disenfranchised. However, Nader suggests that anthropologists also study down because they are uneasy about studying up, or assuming a less powerful position in relationship to the people they study. Nader writes:

> Anthropologists might indeed ask themselves whether the entirety of field work does not depend upon a certain power relationship in favor of the anthropologist, and whether indeed such dominant-subordinate relationships may not be affecting the kinds of theories we are weaving. [1974:289]

Nader had American anthropologists in mind; she also had her own political agenda. Specifically, she called for a study of such institutions as the U.S. Congress. However, the issue of cultural relativism is relevant for all who study their own societies because it goes to the heart of what anthropologists do. The concept of cultural relativism is essential to an understanding of what distinguishes anthropologists from sociologists. According to Murray Leaf (1974), if there is one attitude that deserves to be considered characteristically anthropological, it is cultural relativism.

Michael Agar (1980) notes that as anthropologists increasingly study their own societies, they become more like sociologists. They lose the characteristics that define the field of anthropology. I would argue that we study ourselves with a more critical eye—often more negatively—than we study others, especially if we perceive those others to be disenfranchised and, therefore, nonthreatening.

In doing research in the United States I have studied both down and up. When conducting research among a group of Spiritualists, people who "communicate" with the spirits of the dead, the process was clearly one of studying down. These were people of working-class backgrounds who sought to alleviate their frustrations and anxieties by seeking help from the spirit world. A sense of powerlessness—expressed in metaphors of economics, social relationships, and health—was a primary reason for the existence of the group. People came to the Spiritualist church to get help with their problems. In doing research among professional athletes, on the other hand, I studied up. The athletes had both money and fame and could, by most criteria, be considered a high-status group. Whether they were also powerful is another question entirely.

I found, as did Hortense Powdermaker nearly 30 years before me, that in viewing a group at close range and with reference to other groups, the issue of status and power is more complicated than one might think. In *Stranger and Friend* (1966) Powdermaker reports that in her study of Hollywood actors and actresses, she came to view her famous subjects as powerless victims of a complex social order that included movie producers, directors, and others who made their living through films. She writes: "I saw actors, regardless of their success or wealth, as an underprivileged group; many of them knew they were looked down upon by other members of the Hollywood hierarchy" (1966:227).

Athletes occupy a similar social role. In spite of being the object of public adulation, they are also viewed with contempt as "dumb jocks." Though they make more in one year than most people make in a lifetime, athletes, too, are at the center of a complex social system that includes coaches, team owners, players' agents, and an array of other personnel. Athletes have virtually no control over their daily schedule, key issues involving their health, their future, and, in important ways, their relationships with their families. It is not uncommon for an athlete to find out he has been traded to another team by reading about it in the newspaper, even though being traded will change many aspects of his life. (On one occasion during my study a hockey player learned he had been traded when he was handed an airplane ticket during practice.)

Clearly, athletes are not powerful in relationship to many other members of their organizations. They are, however, more powerful than the anthropologist who studies them. They can refuse to be interviewed and to answer questions and, in extreme cases, can have the anthropologist removed. On the other hand, the anthropologist is powerful in another sense—as a representative of an intellectual establishment that athletes respect or even revere.

If anthropologists are to study up, a great deal more attention must be paid to defining exactly what "up" is. Who really has power in a given society, and what are the realms within which power is exercised? These questions are no less relevant for research in the United States than in studying the Tallensi or the Tiv—and the answers may prove to be surprising. Eric R. Wolf identifies four modes of power:

> One is power as the attribute of the person, as potency or capability. . . . The second kind of power can be understood as the ability of an ego to impose its will on an alter, in social action, in interpersonal relations. . . . [P]ower in the third mode [is] power that controls the settings in which people may show forth their potentialities and interact with others. . . . But there is still a fourth mode of power, power that not only operates within settings or domains but that also organizes and orchestrates the settings themselves, and that specifies the distribution and direction of energy flows. [1990:586]

In all cases, obviously, power is not exercised in a vacuum; the concept of power is meaningful only in the context of social dynamics. In this article the relevant aspect of power is that inherent in the relationship of anthropologist to subjects, as individuals and as groups. When anthropologists are studying people who are less able to impose their will, or to "organize and orchestrate the settings," anthropologists call upon cultural relativism to counteract the imbalance of power. On the other hand, when the people can throw anthropologists out or have them arrested, does cultural relativism continue to be relevant?

To address this question, the concept of cultural relativism must be more clearly defined. Is cultural relativism a methodology or a value system? If it is a methodology—a way of studying human beings that yields reliable data about their behavior—it should be applicable in any context, whether studying up or down. If cultural relativism is a value orientation, it is linked to other values and may or may not be applicable in studying people in positions of power.

Historically, cultural relativism contains elements of both a methodology and a value system. There is little doubt that Franz Boas thought of cultural relativism as a methodology, a way of studying people in other societies with a cultural blindfold. How can we understand others, he asked, if we are unable to step outside our own limited assumptions about what is important? Boas writes:

> The activities of the mind . . . exhibit an infinite variety of form among the peoples of the world. In order to understand these clearly, the student must endeavor to divest himself entirely of opinions and emotions based upon the peculiar social environment into which he is born. [1901:1]

Boas framed this explication of cultural relativism in terms of methodological rigor. On the other hand, he developed his stance in the context of a climate of racial intolerance, and this was a primary concern of his. During Boas's time questions about the relative evolutionary standing of different ethnic groups were considered a valid subject of inquiry. Cultural relativism is an explicit rejection of the idea that the relative worth of different social groups is a valid anthropological issue.

Alison Dundes Renteln argues that cultural relativism, as framed by Boas and applied by his students, was problematic from the beginning because, as she puts it, "they derived an 'ought' from an 'is' " (1988:58). Dundes Renteln adds that, in this context, relativism departs from a theory that describes to one that prescribes. Because relativism is often applied as a value judgment, she argues, the concept is itself ethnocentric:

> Since enculturation leads individuals to prefer their own moral system, the relativist will likewise tend to perceive his own values as superior. What this means is that the relativist prefers tolerance, the value associated with the liberal, democratic tradition. . . . [Tolerance] is simply a value preference of our culture. [1988:63]

What passes for relativism often goes well beyond tolerance to a naive glorification of all that is non-Western. "Cultural relativism" has been transformed into "cultural romanticism." Thus it has provided a rationalization that has allowed anthropologists to make some sweeping generalizations about good and evil, and to use these generalizations as a rationale for judging the value and authenticity of each other's work.

When Colin Turnbull's book *The Mountain People* was published in 1972, it provoked a storm of controversy. Were his data reliable in view of his admitted frustration in working among the Ik? Questions were raised about the appropriateness of portraying the Ik in an unfavorable light. Publication of *The Forest People* in 1962 was not so problematic for anthropologists, in spite of such rhapsodic passages as the following description of the Mbuti Pygmies:

> They were a people who had found in the forest something that made their life more than just worth living, something that made it, with all the hardships and problems and tragedies, a wonderful thing full of joy and happiness and free of care. [Turnbull 1962:26]

Ironically, Turnbull's own data suggest that the lives of the Mbuti are not "free of care." In fact, it appears that the Mbuti believe they must keep careful watch on the forest:

> Moke . . . said, "Normally everything goes well in our world. But at night when we are sleeping, sometimes things go wrong, because we are not awake to stop them from going wrong. Army ants invade the camp; leopards may come in and steal a hunting dog or even a child. If we were awake these things would not happen. So when something big goes wrong, like illness or bad hunting or death, it must be because the forest is sleeping and not looking after its children. So what do we do? We wake it up. We wake it up by singing to it, and we do this because we want it to awaken happy. Then everything will be well and good again. So when our world is going well then also we sing to the forest because we want it to share our happiness." [1962:92]

As this passage indicates, Mbuti songs are not a simple expression of "joy and happiness"; they are also a form of protection against the dangers of living in the forest. Of course, the relevant point here is not whether or not the Mbuti are happy and carefree, but why anthropologists react so differently to equally subjective assessments of other people's emotional and moral life. Why do anthropologists react with censure when they hear about a group of people driven to the extremes of survival as a result of laws restricting them from access to their former territory as in the case of the Ik, but accept with credulity a report of a people singing happy songs as they go about their work in the forest?

On another level, Napoleon Chagnon has been criticized for his description of the Yanomamo as "the fierce people" (1968). It has been suggested that he projected his own hostilities onto the people he studied. The issue in itself is a valid one. As human beings studying human beings, anthropologists are susceptible to distortions caused by their own experiences of the world. Yet it is debatable whether Chagnon would have attracted such a degree of criticism if he had described the Yanomamo as "gentle" or "harmless," even though all these terms reflect value judgments.

Kenneth Good takes Chagnon to task for his description of the Yanomamo as "fierce," noting:

> Raiding, killing, and wife beating all happened; I was seeing it, and no doubt I'd see a lot more of it. But by misrepresenting violence as the central theme of Yanomamo life, his *Fierce People* book had blown the subject out of any sane proportion. [1991:73]

With some accuracy, Good argues that calling the Yanomamo the "fierce people" is equivalent to calling New Yorkers "the mugging and murdering people."

An essential point underlying the debate is whether the complexity of sociocultural life can be summed up by any single adjective. When people describe themselves in adjectival terms, they are using a strategy to obscure differences among them and picture themselves in a positive light. Describing others in adjectival terms is often used to denigrate them. For example, the New Yorkers whom Good suggests could be described as "the mugging and murdering people" might designate themselves as "the sophisticated people." In both cases, such simplistic designations are strategies aimed at positioning oneself with reference to an "other" or an "alter," to use Wolf's term. As James Fernandez notes in his discussion of metaphor: "The strategy is to make it appear that the incumbent occupies a desirable or undesirable place in the continuum of whatever domain has been chosen" (1971:45).

At issue is whether anthropological participation in the process of metaphorical positioning of different societies with reference to each other is compatible with the ethnographic enterprise. Ironically, Boas conceived of cultural relativism as a tool to avoid value judgments; it now appears to have become a tool in the service of political positioning.

Several anthropologists with whom I discussed an early draft of this article remarked that it is "safer" to portray the people they study in a favorable light. This suggests that ethnography with a positive slant is perceived as more easily published and less likely to be harshly criticized. It could be revealing to ascertain how widespread this perception is and whether it imparts a Panglossian bias to anthropological reports. Do anthropologists perceive their role as that of benevolent observers with the power to award a stamp of approval to the people they study and proclaim their lifestyle the best of all possible worlds? If so, this perception must surely be challenged in the process of studying up.

The inherently patronizing tone of such terms as "harmless" or "gentle" becomes readily apparent if applied to members of a powerful group like the U.S. Senate. Turnbull described the Mbuti pygmies as "simple" and "unaffected" (1962:23). Would he consider such labels flattering if applied to himself? Would Senator Ted Kennedy or activist Gloria Steinem or athlete Kareem Abdul-Jabbar find such descriptions of themselves appealing? Terms such as "harmless" and "gentle" are commonly applied to people who are in a nonthreatening or subordinate position; they are never used to designate people who are in a position to act decisively and effectively.

It may be argued that the use of diminutive labels is a benign form of paternalism. However, cultural romanticism may actually result in harm to the people anthropologists study. Joan Weibel-Orlando notes that anthropologists studying substance abuse among Native Americans consistently favor indigenous healing mechanisms over mainstream techniques of intervention in the absence of data to support such a stance:

> We suspect mainstream intervention modalities as being inherently not culture sensitive and workable among post-tribal peoples. We assume our advocacy is welcomed by the people whose cause we champion and whose right to choose their own interventions we view as inviolate. [1988:11]

It is likely that the anthropological role as apologist for "traditional" or "tribal" societies is rooted in the uncomfortable position anthropologists traditionally occupy as participant-observers in colonialism. It allows them to resolve moral conflicts by disassociating themselves from the encroaching colonial power and identifying with the people who are being disempowered. As Weibel-Orlando implies, however, this identification may not be welcomed by the people anthropologists study.

A number of authors have argued that cultural relativism has resulted in a kind of valueless philosophy, one in which all ideas and all systems are viewed as equivalent. Dundes Renteln rejects this view. Relativism, she writes, says nothing about the desirability of social criticism:

> It holds that every society will utilize its own standards. Sometimes there will be a fundamental conflict among the various standards. What one makes of the conflicting or consensual standards depends not on relativism but on the role one wishes to play in the international community. [1988:64]

Anthropologists cannot escape their position in the power dynamic resulting from the relationship between "traditional" people and an encroaching global culture by hiding behind cultural romanticism. Studying up reveals the attempt to be both untenable and, in many cases, a disservice to the people anthropologists study. Is, then, cultural relativism a relic of colonialism?

Gananath Obeyesekere argues that the issue of cultural relativism could be resolved if anthropologists focused on methodological relativism rather than philosophical relativism. He writes: "Methodological relativism asserts that it may be a useful procedure for the social sciences to view morals and customs as if they were relative for certain scientific purposes" (1966:371). Obeyesekere asserts that relativism as a methodology supports a value free science and "dispenses with the need to have value judgments anchored in some law of science" (1966:371). He echoes Boas by noting that a "methodological relativism obviates ethnocentrism" (1966:371).

Just as philosophical relativists appear too ready to turn away from methodological relativism, Obeyesekere too easily dismisses philosophical relativism and seems to overlook the connection between the two. As noted above, romanticism masquerading as relativism often finds its way into methodology, in that anthropologists frame their questions, conduct their studies, and construct explanations in the rosy light of romanticism. In this regard relativism does not, in fact, obviate ethnocentrism. Rather, it gives rise to a different form of ethnocentrism. It does not, as Boas claimed, remove our cultural blindfolds; it merely replaces them with rose-colored glasses.

Rigorously applied, however, cultural relativism has great value as a methodology. It does not simply eliminate harsh judgments of people with customs and values different from our own; it also provides a context for framing research questions in our own society. This was demonstrated repeatedly in my work among professional athletes.

Anthropologists fear prejudging people with social customs that are largely unfamiliar to them. However, the danger of prejudging is even greater when studying people we think we know. During my study of athletes I was bombarded with value judgments from a plethora of mass media and from my own acquaintances, as well as from my own expectations. Everyone, it seems, is an "expert" on sports. Only by actively refusing to prejudge was I able to bypass the pseudo-experts and focus on the real experts—the athletes themselves.

Cultural relativism also proves its worth in the context of applied anthropology. Some years ago I was asked to evaluate an academic program viewed as problematic by the administration of a large university. I was given the following instructions: Find out what is wrong with the program and recommend whether it should be eliminated. The project became for me an opportunity to test traditional anthropological methodology in a complex society. In keeping with methodological cultural relativism, I had to rephrase the research question. "What is wrong with this group?" was translated into a series of questions familiar to anthropologists: "How is this group organized economically and politically, both internally and with reference to other groups?" "How does it define itself?" "What does it consider important?"

The essential anthropological question—"Who are you and what do you think you are doing?"—is often skipped in conducting research in our own society because we assume we know the answer. And that is a fatal error. It is the unique contribution of anthropology that we do not assume we have some kind of superior knowledge of the people we study. We have to ask the experts—the people themselves. It is a contribution made possible by cultural relativism.

"Who are you and what do you think you are doing?" provided the key to my study of the ailing academic group, which, I discovered, lacked a sense of purpose. The program had started out as a good idea but had evolved into a bureaucratic anomaly that existed merely to exist. As with the Ik, the program's overriding purpose was survival and its primary activity was competing for resources. Out of this grew a host of problems, including hostile relations with other campus entities.

One of the most striking findings of my study, from the perspective of testing anthropological methodology, is that scholars from a number of disciplines agreed the report identified every variable that had been subjectively considered a problem for the program. In other words, my ethnography of the program withstood the test of intersubjectivity. Anthropologists sometimes worry that their methods will produce results that will not hold up when subjected to the scrutiny of less maverick disciplines. This did not prove to be the case.

I do not share the concern of some anthropologists that our tools—including cultural relativism—are not up to the task of studying complex societies. On the contrary, they are the best ones for the job. However, we are going to have to keep our tools clean and well polished, free of the accumulated debris of too many years of cultural romanticism.

Studying up, however, presents some challenges of its own. In conducting research among the rich and powerful, the anthropologist must get used to the role of "hanger on" and to the complex sentiments this engenders. The aura of power is seductive. On the other hand, one can be banished from the kingdom at a moment's notice. All these subtle and not-so-subtle influences have important implications for maintaining a stance of methodological relativism. Anthropologists can become ego-involved with their position in the power dynamics of any group. In studying down, anthropologists tend to overcompensate for their equivocal role by romanticizing the people they study. In studying up it is hard to distance oneself from the ambivalent emotions one feels toward those in positions of greater power.

Anthropologists have developed methods that allow them to function in environments where the rules are unfamiliar. As we return now to do research in surroundings that appear to be familiar and well understood, it is important not to lose the perspective that will allow us to look with a sense of discovery at our own institutions. That is, a perspective aided by cultural relativism in its rigorous methodological form.

References Cited

Agar, Michael
1980 The Professional Stranger. New York: Academic Press.
Boas, Franz
1901 The Mind of Primitive Man. Journal of American Folklore 13:1–11.
Chagnon, Napoleon A.
1968 Yanomamo: The Fierce People. New York: Holt, Rinehart and Winston.
Dundes Renteln, Alison
1988 Relativism and the Search for Human Rights. American Anthropologist 90:56–72.
Fernandez, James W.
1971 Persuasions and Performances: Of the Beast in Every Body . . . and the Metaphors of Everyman. *In* Myth, Symbol and Culture. Clifford Geertz, ed. Pp. 39–60. New York: Norton.
Good, Kenneth (with David Chanoff)
1991 Into the Heart: One Man's Pursuit of Love and Knowledge among the Yanomamo. New York: Simon and Schuster.
Leaf, Murray
1974 Frontiers of Anthropology. New York: Van Nostrand.

Nader, Laura
1974 Up the Anthropologist: Perspectives Gained from Studying Up. *In* Reinventing Anthropology. Dell Hymes, ed. Pp. 284–311. New York: Vintage Books.
Obeyesekere, Gananath
1966 Methodological and Philosophical Relativism. Man 1:368–374.
Powdermaker, Hortense
1966 Stranger and Friend: The Way of an Anthropologist. New York: Norton.
Turnbull, Colin
1962 The Forest People. New York: Touchstone.
1972 The Mountain People. New York: Touchstone.
Weibel-Orlando, Joan
1988 Hooked on Healing: Anthropologists, Alcohol and Intervention. Newsletter of the Alcohol and Drug Study Group of the American Anthropological Association 21:10–19.
Wolf, Eric R.
1990 Distinguished Lecture: Facing Power—Old Insights, New Questions. American Anthropologist 92:586–596.

Anthropology and the Oppressed: A Reflection on "Native" Anthropology

Delmos J. Jones

In my article "Towards a Native Anthropology" (Jones 1970) I expressed my frustration and dissatisfaction with the social-class and racial bias of anthropology. What concerned me then, as now, is that anthropology is essentially a discipline that studies oppressed peoples, but the concepts and theories used to describe the lives of these groups do not adequately deal with the realities of their oppression. Thus I could just as well have called for an anthropology of the oppressed. Although my subsequent writings have not directly addressed the topic of a "native" anthropology, most of them have dealt with issues of domination and oppression.

The idea that members of an oppressed group become anthropologists is an important dimension of the relationship between anthropology, native anthropology, and the oppressed. Thus there are three problems that must be addressed: anthropology as a discipline, the native anthropologist as an individual, and the socioeconomic status of the population that the native anthropologist belongs to. The relationship between the native anthropologist and the native population is not self-evident, although it often is made to appear that way. That is, the anthropologist who is a member of an oppressed population may or may not be an advocate of an anthropology of the oppressed. The relationship of the individual to the discipline may have more of an impact on point of view than his or her membership in a specific population. This issue is a major topic of this article.

My primary concern is neither anthropology nor native anthropology. Rather, it is social equality and social justice, and the manner in which anthropology and native anthropology relate to these concerns. I am referring here to the often stated idea that anthropology has provided justification for colonialism and oppression. With this principle in mind, native anthropology must be subjected to the same level of scrutiny as mainstream anthropology. The central question is whether a native anthropology advances the goals of social justice and social equality, or whether it merely mirrors mainstream anthropology. I will argue that some perspectives presented as critiques of mainstream anthropology are often no different from the point of view they are criticizing. Thus I agree with Narayan's recent argument (1993) against the fixity of a sharp distinction between native and "nonnative" anthropology. However, I would go on to suggest that there should be a distinction. Narayan is critical of the idea that a "native anthropologist" can represent an unproblematic and authentic "insider's perspective" on social reality. I would suggest that there are political implications to this claim. This claim tends to deny the multiple voices of the native population for whom the native anthropologist purports to speak, and may serve to legitimize internal inequality.

In this article I will describe a research situation where I encountered the issues of multiple commitments and loyalties, where social class, race, and political ideology converged in contradictory ways. This incident will show that there is no one-to-one relationship between an insider researcher and a local population. Rather, all relationships involving research are problematic, socially and politically complex, and require difficult choices. My argument is that if these choices are based on sentimentality as opposed to political considerations, they risk reinforcing inequality. The native anthropologist must be seen in relationship to a native population, but the native population must not be viewed as a homogeneous and cohesive entity. It is composed of diverse interests. The native anthropologist must also be seen in connection to the discipline of anthropology, and anthropology must be seen as an economic undertaking, and also an academic one. Finally, anthropology and native anthropology must be seen in a wider social and political context.

Native Anthropology, 1970–1995

When I called for a native anthropology, I had in mind a process that would transform anthropology very much in the manner that feminist studies has since achieved to some extent. The most productive advance in this direction is *Decolonizing Anthropology* (Harrison 1991). As Harrison put it, there is a need for an anthropology concerned about the struggle against racist oppression, gender inequality, class disparities, and international patterns of exploitation.

The starting point for "Towards a Native Anthropology" was the notion that the manner in which an object is observed depends upon the position from which it is viewed. Logically, an adequate description of any phenomenon should involve observations from more than one position. In the social sciences, where the observer is a human being, relative position must include factors such as race, gender, and social class. Black Americans, other nonwhite populations in the United States, and the people of most Third World countries share a history of colonization and other forms of domination. This domination is rooted largely in racial, ethnic, and cultural differences.

Every perspective has its own limitations. While being part of a parade may not be the best vantage point to observe the whole parade, an observer who has been part of a parade undoubtedly has a different insight because of that experience. Thus it was my view that an individual who has experienced domination and oppression could probably add a new dimension to the anthropological description of oppressed people.

In the years since the publication of my piece on native anthropology I have had plenty of time to reflect on what I would now say differently about the topic. Then I wrote: "[A] black man in this century cannot avoid identifying emotionally with his people. I am an intrinsic part of the social situation that I am attempting to study. As part of the situation, I must also be part of an attempt to forge a solution" (1970:255). This remains the case. However, on reflection I would now suggest that an important distinction should be made among commitments to one's people, commitment to ideas about one's people, and commitment to political goals for one's people. I now have more to say about the idea of "one's people," in the sense that this phrase is taken to refer to a some kind of homogeneous collective.

I wrote that "the native anthropologist should be one who looks at social phenomena from a point of view different from that of the traditional anthropologist. I feel that this point of view should be admittedly biased, in favor of the insider's own social group" (1970:258). The expression "admittedly biased" was an unfortunate choice of words as much as it appears to give license to tell untruths. The phrase "in favor of the insider's own social group" is ambiguous. Since different, and sometimes conflicting, interests exist in most social groups, it is not always clear just whose interests are being served. When diverse interests exist the native researcher must decide among them, and that decision should be based on political considerations. Primordial loyalty to a racial or ethnic "group" is no substitute for political goals. I believe that embracing a wider political agenda will free one from the destructive tendency to be loyal to one's own group, "right or wrong."

In "Towards a Native Anthropology" I criticized the cohesive model of society that was, and still is, expressed in much of the anthropological literature. Yet the concept of "one's own group" is merely another version of the same model. It is in this context that Marcus and Fischer's (1986) critique of Edward Said is relevant. They note that Said "acknowledged no political or cultural division among the subject people he is allegedly defending. They have no more independent voice in his text than in that of Western writers" (1986:2). The failure to acknowledge political and cultural divisions within a group can become an aspect of domination.

The "insiders' own social group," in my case black Americans, are not the only oppressed people in the United States, and there is a relationship between the socioeconomic status of black Americans and other oppressed peoples. However, there is a tendency for native anthropologists to be primarily concerned with an improvement in the life conditions of their "own people," however this group is defined. This has led to a "culturally specific," even a nationalistic, perspective on social reality (see Gerholm and Hannerz 1982).

If I favored subjectivity over objectivity it is because I believe it to be virtually impossible to escape what Calverton (1931:28–29) called "cultural compulsives." However, native anthropologists are not free from cultural compulsives (Gerholm and Hannerz 1982), and they may fall into the same type of ideological and political traps as traditional anthropologists. Moreover, there is the risk that the native anthropologist may confuse his or her status in the discipline with changes in the status quo. This, I suspect, is Narayan's error. The person who has experienced discrimination and oppression but has achieved some advancement can choose how relevant that experience is. I am especially worried insofar as the improved status of the native anthropologist is based upon the subordinate status and cultural difference of the population that the native anthropologist is a member of. Indigenous elites often benefit from the inequality that exists within a group. Kilson's (1989) discussion of a "self-serving elite" among black Americans refers to the capital mobilization and formulation that have taken place for an expanding black capitalist sector, a development that has benefited a small segment of the black middle and upper-middle class at the expense of the working class and poor blacks. It is in this context that we must inspect the claim that only the insider researcher can understand the culture of a group. Not only does this assertion lay claim to a resource, information about the group, but it is also anchored in very common ideas about the nature of culture.

It was Madan (1982) who noted that the native or indigenous anthropologist has a stake in the nature of his society and that he must, therefore, become an agent of social change, give a push to history in a particular desired direction. Unlike the outsider, he cannot afford the luxury of a value-free social science. He is not a dispassionate observer of a social scene, but an active player in it. It is this multiple role of observer and potential actor, which makes the role of the indigenous anthropologist so problematic. What is the nature of the proposed action? Just who has decided that course of action among all other possible courses? Was it the anthropologist? The state? A political elite? What is its context in the social and political order? Who will benefit most from the proposed action? Political action is not always one-directional, against an "outside" authority, but may sometimes be directed against segments of the native population. Morauta (1979), for example, suggested that the indigenous anthropologist in New Guinea works mainly in the service of the national elite of the society. The idea of cultural unity in New Guinea, as summed up in the expression "the Melanesian way," is an expression that denotes "a kind of super tribe concept," a slogan popular with the national elite, but "which may serve to distract attention from the growing economic and political inequalities between regions and classes within Papua New Guinea" (Morauta 1979:13). It is in this context that Gerholm and Hannerz noted that "national anthropologists, no less than world anthropologists, can have their centers and their periphery" (1982:21). It is also in this context that Madan warns of the dangers of anthropology's being incorporated into the state (1982:15).

Madan was speaking of the anthropologists in Third World nation-states. There is a similar problem in pluralistic Western societies where the anthropologist is a member of an ethnic or minority group and the relationship is between the anthropologist and a minority population. Here the anthropologist may have to guard against becoming the intellectual prisoner of an ethnic elite. Thus it was proposed that "urban ethnographers must agree readily to the boundaries of investigation as decided by ghetto nationalists" (Willis 1972:148). To agree to such restrictions without reflection would be an act of blind loyalty. It would not necessarily be loyalty to the group as to a segment of the group, with the assumption that this segment is acting in the best interest of the whole. The degree to which loyalty to a particular segment of a group is the same as loyalty to the group depends upon the nature of the particular segment, and its relationship to the larger population. It is because of this that this relationship itself must be subjected to scrutiny.

Group loyalty in various forms is something that native anthropologists must contend with, and peer pressure is applied to achieve it. At the 1969 annual meeting of the Society for Applied Anthropologists, Vera Green, a black anthropologist, delivered a paper, "The Confrontation of Diversity in the Black Community." It was published the next year in *Human Organization* (Green 1970). A major criticism made of this paper was that she should not have discussed the internal diversity that exists in the black community. The face of black unity should be presented no matter what the nature of the internal problems. Green was describing the negative political implication of ignoring the internal diversity that exists. Wilson (1987) writes about this problem in relationship to studies of the poor. He concluded that by 1970 research on the "ghetto underclass" had to be research conducted by minority scholars on the strengths, not the weaknesses, of inner-city families and communities (Wilson 1987:15). I have argued elsewhere that this antipathological approach was just as inadequate as the position it was criticizing. The tone of much of this writing is more oppositional than transformative, more didactic than descriptive, and often embraces the same theoretical framework as the one seemingly being opposed (see Jones 1993).

In the following section I will describe a research situation in which I encountered the issues of multiple commitments and localities of a native anthropologist working with a native population. I will describe how my research agenda related to different segments of the group, and how each segment had different expectations. As a native anthropologist I had to make a choice. The nature of my choices was not based on my "nativeness," but on political and ideological grounds.

The Research Case

In most of my research I have emphasized the study of voluntary associations or local organizations. This is due to a concern with the interaction between the institutions of power and minority populations (see Jones 1972, 1976, 1980, 1987). It is primarily through organizations that an oppressed population attempts to bring about changes in its condition, but it is also through organizations that the state attempts to control urban populations. In a study conducted in 1968 on the origin and function of community organizations, I observed many aborted attempts at developing organizations, which rarely survived the incipient stage (see Jones 1972). Questions arose about the conditions that lead to failure or success in organizations. The research pointed to a process that was channeling the direction of political development in the black community by deciding the types of organizations that survived (see Arnstein 1972).

A second study, carried out between 1972 and 1973, focused on a "successful" organization, often touted as an example of what could be accomplished by local associations. According to my analysis, the group was successful because its goals, the development of low-income housing, coincided with the goals of the city's housing authority. To be successful, it appeared, an organization had to have a leadership that was acceptable to the community, and one that government agencies could do business with. Thus the leader of local organizations must respond to the demands and expectations of external agencies, and attempt to remain acceptable to the local community. The interest of these two groups, however, are often contradictory.

The study of the Community Action Group was designed to look in more detail inside an organization and to investigate the consequences of antagonistic elements—the interests of the state and the interests of the poor—locked into the same organizational structure. The patterns of social interaction between leaders and followers, and the relationship between the organization as a unit and the people of the larger community were the primary concerns of this research.

The Community Action Group operated a Head Start Center and emerged out of the atmosphere of the war on poverty and the Black Power ideology of the late 1960s (see Jones 1987). Like most organizations of this type, the group consisted of a board of directors, the governing and policy-making body of the organization; a working staff, including professionals and paraprofessionals; and clients, people from the community who received services offered by the organization.

While planning the study I appeared before the full board of directors. They carefully inspected my political views and asked specific questions about my proposed study. I was granted permission to do the study, partly because the board approved of my political concern about the position of black people, and because I am black. A white researcher would not have been allowed to do the study. As a condition of this approval, I was asked by the board to meet occasionally with them to report my findings. They explained that the organization was experiencing many internal problems and that my investigation might help them to solve them.

Being black was not enough in this all-black organization. The social class dimensions of my identity emerged immediately (see Mitchell 1982:31 for a similar experience). The manner in which I gained entry into the group was the source of my first problem. I had received permission from the board to conduct the research, but the research itself took place at the center among parents and a paraprofessional staff who had no voice in that decision. Thus when I started the research there was immediate suspicion by the parents and staff about who I was and what I was doing. Was I working for the central office, the city agency in charge of all city Head Start programs, as part of their monitoring team? Was I working for the board, collecting information they would use to fire the staff?

By the time I appeared on the scene the board had decided that the whole staff was inefficient and needed replacing; the staff, hiding behind the protection of community support and formal grievance procedures, was able to protect their jobs. Although most performed at a minimal level, most of them also reported a history of hard work and commitment to the job. They complained that their commitment and hard work went unrewarded. The board wanted to get rid of the staff, and the dominant sentiment of the parents was to get rid of the board.

Although I was asked at the beginning of the project to appear before the board to relate the findings of my research, I was not invited to do so until the study was completed and the analysis underway. When I did come before the board I gave an oral report in which I discussed the issues as outlined above. The report was politely received, and a written report was requested. When the written report was submitted to the board, the chairperson felt that the findings were all wrong and urged that it not be shown to anyone else in the organization. I was invited to reappear before the board to discuss the accuracy of the written report. I agreed.

I happened to mention the meeting to a board member. She was very surprised and said she had never heard of the meeting. When she looked into it, she discovered that the meeting was to involve me and the board's top leadership. This upset her, and when I understood that this was to be a meeting of a few select board members I refused to attend it. I was willing to discuss the accuracy of the report, but only before the full board.

News of the affair quickly spread. Everyone knew that a report had been written, and the staff and parents learned that they were not supposed to see it. I was now watched very closely. When I first came into the organization, I was suspected by the staff of working for the board. Would I now prove to be on the board's side? The report was seen by the board as an authoritarian document that would serve to support the position of the leadership against the parents and staff, but it was seen by the parents and staff as a statement that would discredit the board.

I decided to circulate the report in the organization over the objection of the leadership. This decision was not an easy one. It was based in part on my realization that parents and staff had a right to see my interpretation of their experience. As I struggled with the problem of what to do about the report, ideas associated with my role as a black anthropologist working in a black social situation were uppermost in my mind. I wish now to discuss some of these issues.

Contradictions and Dilemmas

I started this line of research by raising political questions. I was concerned about the decline of politically viable organizations and their substitutions with organizations devoted to providing services. I was asking questions about the manipulation and control of black organizations and, indirectly, the control of leadership and political action. When the wider context of the problem is confronted, the relationship between leaders and followers among black Americans emerges as a core part of the problem. It was Marable who noted that "the Black petty bourgeoisie . . . express tendencies toward political accommodation and class collaboration with the state" (1981:373). Marable went on to note that "part of the crisis in Black politics involves the breakdown in Black leadership" (1981:377; see also Karenga 1982:19). It is in this context that the role of the native anthropologist as ethnographer-critic and as a member of a minority group becomes problematic (see Mitchell 1982). Should the native researcher, in the name of group loyalty, fail to report socially destructive aspects of the native situation?

In my case I experienced a conflict between the political concerns that I was investigating and my personal sentiments about the idea of black unity. In my report to the board I made every effort to reveal the external roots of the internal conflict. However, I implicitly advocated unity. At the same time, the findings of the research suggested that the racial unity ideology was creating many of the interpersonal problems in the organization. This was because the idea of unity was often a device to suppress meaningful social, ideological, and political difference.

The Community Action Group case was a microcosm of a larger political and ideological scene in the United States during 1965–76. This was a period characterized by an ideology that stressed the organization of the black community as a precondition for wedging an attack on the oppressive conditions of society (Carmichael and Hamilton 1967:44–45). In the Community Action Group, for example, any discussion of social differences was viewed as inappropriate behavior resulting from "white brainwashing." Any suggestion that the leadership was anything but fully and totally committed to legitimate political goals and not out for their personal gain was called anti-black. Thus the situation lacked any kind of exchange between leaders and followers. Communications took the form of memorandums from the board to the rest of the organization. The group as a whole no longer mobilized to confront the policies of the central office and other outside institutions. Rather, the parents mobilized the community against the board (see Jones 1987 for a more detailed description of this topic), and the leadership spent a lot of effort trying to keep the parents in line.

The idea of unity in this situation meant that the parents would follow the dictates of the leadership without question. The more I examined the idea of unity the more it appeared that the notion that a black community could or should be built was more primordial than political, based more on principles of racial loyalty than on a specific political agenda, and functioned more to domesticate than to liberate.

In the oral report I implicitly advocated racial unity. In doing so I, along with central office personnel, did not acknowledge the parents' legitimacy as political actors who had characterized the leadership as the oppressors, and had decided that they no longer wanted to accept the structure as given. It is in the context of this realization that Paulo Freire's *Pedagogy of the Oppressed* (1970) became important to me. In his discussion of critical intervention he stressed "dialoguing with people about their actions" (1970:38–39) and noted that to substitute monologue, slogans, and communiqués for dialogue is to attempt to liberate the oppressed with the instruments of domestication.

> Attempting to liberate the oppressed without their reflective participation in the act of liberation is to treat them as objects which must be saved from a burning building; it is to lead them into the populist pitfall and transform them into masses which can be manipulated. [Freire 1970:52]

Freire would give a voice to the oppressed and subject the relationship between the oppressed and their would-be liberators to critical analysis. It is not a relationship that is self-evident, but one that must be earned and revalidated over and over again (see Stavenhagen 1971). It is also in this context that the statement "urban ethnographers must agree readily to the boundaries of investigation as decided by ghetto nationalists" (Willis 1972:148) must be rejected.

Conclusion

I began this article with the comment that my primary concern is not anthropology or native anthropology, but social equality and social justice. I complained that the concepts and theories used to describe the life of oppressed groups do not adequately deal with the realities of that oppression. The primary issue is not one of identity, whether the anthropologist is a "native," but one of content, the nature of the descriptive discourse. Thus the writings of the native anthropologist must also be subjected to scrutiny. Both mainstream and native anthropologists operate in a social and political context. They can be placed in the service of the state or become captive of a native elite. Consequently, in both cases political judgments are required, and these judgments should be made with respect to the larger question of social justice and social equality.

Narayan implies that because anthropology is currently practiced by Third World and minority anthropologists, the discipline's ethnocentric formulations have been realigned or overthrown (1993:673). I have suggested that the opposite may well be the case. My argument is that the ideas presented by Third World and minority anthropologists are often more oppositional than transformative and actually embrace the same perspective as those found in mainstream anthropology. For example, the "sun" people verses "ice" people discussion (see Bradley 1978) is a modern-day reversal of 19th-century biological and environmental determinism. The school of thought that has dominated research on the black Americans for more than three decades (see Hare 1970) is characterized by what Oliver Cox (1970) calls the black bourgeoisie school of thought. An intriguing notion of this school, according to Cox, "is that Negro institutions and practices are largely 'make believe.' " Implicit in this perspective, Cox writes, is that when the "Negro middle class abandoned the lower class culture, . . . they are then bereft of all culture" (1970:16–18).

It is necessary to inspect the theory of culture, cultural change, and cultural transmission implied in this position. Stripped of its racial context, this view is consistent with the principles of genuine and spurious culture as advocated by Sapir (1924). It is a perspective that emphasizes the persistence of traditional cultural practices. Traditional cultures either do not change or should not change. Indigenous people in state systems are described in cultural terms, and the persistence of traditional cultural practices is considered apart from the issue of domination. The persistence of traditional cultural practices in the context of modern states is even equated with resistance against domination and oppression. Cultural differences are often associated with social and economic inequality. However, in much of the anthropological literature, "the relationship of exploitation to culture is either ignored or made completely subsidiary to the study of 'culture' as abstracted from the exploitative reality" (Caulfield 1972:185).

I have suggested that in the Community Action Group situation the notion of unity was used to suppress dissent. Additionally, there was the tendency to submerge internal social and individual differences. This emphasis on the group, defined largely in cultural terms, as opposed to the rights of the individual, is currently an important political and moral issue. It is embedded in the debate between communitarians and liberals, and is an important aspect of discussions about universal human rights (Buchanan 1989; Rawles 1971; Tomasi 1991; Van Dyke 1982, 1985). Bromley points out that when the Universal Declaration of Human Rights was under discussion at the United Nations in the 1940s, a report was issued by the American Anthropological Association attempting to establish "on the basis of cultural relativism, that there could be no general human rights for all people" (1987:33). This idea that all ethnic cultures are relative leads to the conclusion that each culture has a permanent value and must be preserved for as long as possible in its "pure" form. The result, however well intended, is the perpetuation of the existing inequality within groups and between groups. From this perspective, groups are not only more important than individuals, but should and must limit individual freedom and action, and such restrictions are inherently justified.

There is much in the general anthropological literature to suggest that at the level of cultural authenticity, issues of inequality and oppression do not exist (Bromley 1987). There is no such thing as power, the quest for power, or the abuse of power. Most accounts of what Meadwell (1989) describes as expressive culturalism emphasize culture, depend on methodological holism, and play down internal differences. "Individuals are defined by their structural location in cultures and individual identity is exhausted by their position" (Meadwell 1989:311–312). "People are born into a given category and cannot escape it; and certain rights, eligibilities, and opportunities depend on the category in which they find themselves" (Van Dyke 1985:101). Thus the suppression of dissent is justified on primordial grounds, and primordialism is elevated to the highest possible moral status.

Most of my thinking about social issues has been guided by an appreciation for social complexity and the strategic and destructive nature of capitalism. I am suspicious of discussions of neighborhood "self-help," indigenous community development, neighborhood "preservation," "community control," "self determination," "cultural resistance," and "empowerment." These developments are attempts to deal with conditions created by capitalistic processes. However, most discussions of these topics assume that they can be successful without a drastic transformation of capitalism. I have also been attuned to what Fanon calls the problem of identity and cultural consciousness in an exploitative situation (quoted in Caulfield 1972:188), and what Trent Schroyer (1973) described as the difficulty of achieving a revolutionary consciousness in a society where an enormous amount of time and effort is exerted by the state to control and manipulate consciousness. I ended "Towards a Native Anthropology" calling for the decolonization of anthropological knowledge. It should now be clear to everyone that decolonization is not always the same thing as liberation, especially if the process only replaces one system of domination with another. Schroyer (1973) noted that "contemporary establishment social science is essentially a science of managerial rationality." He called for a science capable of recognizing the ways in which existing structures exploit, alienate, and repress human possibilities. "We need a critical science whose primary focus is the critique of domination" (1973:27). This critique must not stop at the boundaries of minorities and oppressed populations, conceived as cohesive wholes, but must recognize that mechanisms of domination and exploitation operate at all levels of social reality. It is because of this that a critical native anthropology is now needed more than ever.

The idea that a native anthropology does not represent an "unproblematic perspective" on social reality does not diminish the potential of a transformative anthropology. Mitchell, for example, asks: "[H]ow does one objectively study a population considered 'deviant' when the researchers themselves, although considered exceptions, are members of that deviant population?" (1982:42). It is precisely by confronting, analyzing, and working through the multiple social realities, dilemmas, constraints, and choices that native anthropologists participate in as actors and observers that the potential rewards of the undertaking exist.

References Cited

Arnstein, S. R.
1972 Maximum Feasible Manipulation. Public Administration Review 32:377–403.

Bradley, Michael
1978 The Iceman Inheritance: Prehistoric Sources of Western Man's Racism, Sexism and Aggression. New York: Kayode Publishing.

Bromley, Yu V.
1987 Anthropology, Ethnology and Ethnic and Racial Prejudice. International Social Science Journal 39:31–43.

Buchanan, Allen E.
1989 Assessing the Communitarian Critique of Liberalism. Ethics 99:852–882.

Calverton, V. F.
1931 The Making of Man: An Outline of Anthropology. New York: Modern Library.

Carmichael, Stokey, and Charles Hamilton
1967 Black Power. New York: Random House.

Caulfield, N. D.
1972 Culture and Imperialism: Proposing a New Dialectic. *In* Reinventing Anthropology. Dell Hymes, ed. Pp. 182–212. New York: Random House.

Cox, Oliver
1970 Introduction. *In* The Black Anglo-Saxons, by Nathan Hare. Pp. 15–31. London: Collier-Macmillan.

Freire, Paolo
1970 Pedagogy of the Oppressed. New York: Seabury Press.

Gerholm, Tomas, and Ulf Hannerz
1982 Introduction: The Shaping of National Anthropologies. Ethnos 47:1–32

Green, Vera
1970 The Confrontation of Diversity within the Black Community. Human Organization 29:207–227.

Hare, Nathan
1970 The Black Anglo-Saxons. London: Collier-Macmillan.

Harrison, Faye V.
1991 Anthropology as an Agent of Transformation: Introductiory Comments and Queries. *In* Decolonizing Anthropology. Faye V. Harrison, ed. Pp. 1–14. Washington, DC: American Anthropological Association.

Jones, Delmos J.
1970 Towards a Native Anthropology. Human Organization 29:251–259.
1972 Incipient Organizations and Organizational Failures in an Urban Ghetto. Urban Anthropology 1:51–67.
1976 Applied Anthropology and the Application of Anthropological Knowledge. Human Organization 35:221–230.

1980 Accountability and the Politics of Urban Research. Human Organization 39:99–104.
1987 The Community and Organizations in the Community. *In* Anthropology in the United States. Leith Mullings, ed. Pp. 115–136. New York: Columbia University Press.
1993 The Culture of Achievement among the Poor: The Case of Mothers and Children in a Head Start Program. Critique of Anthropology 13(3):247–266.
Karenga, Maulana
1982 Crisis of Black Middle Class Leadership: A Critical Analysis. Black Scholar 13:16–32.
Kilson, Milton
1989 Problems of Black Politics: Some Progress, Many Difficulties. Dissent (Fall):526–535.
Madan, T. N.
1982 Anthropology as the Mutual Interpretation of Cultures: Indian Perspectives. *In* Indigenous Anthropology in Non-Western Countries. Hussein Fahim, ed. Pp. 4–18. Durham, NC: Carolina Academic Press.
Marable, Manning
1981 Reaganism, Racism, and Reaction: Black Political Realignment. Black Scholar 13:2–15.
Marcus, George E., and Michael M. J. Fisher
1986 Anthropology as Cultural Critique. Chicago: University of Chicago Press.
Meadwell, Hudson
1989 Cultural and Instrumental Approaches to Ethnic Nationalism. Ethnic and Racial Studies 12(3):309–388.
Mitchell, Jacquelyn
1982 Reflections of a Black Social Scientist: Some Struggles, Some Doubts, Some Hopes. Harvard Educational Review 52:27–44.
Morauta, L.
1979 Indigenous Anthropology in Papua New Guinea. Gigibori 4(2):4–14.
Narayan, Kirin
1993 How Native is a "Native" Anthropologist? American Anthropologist 95:671–686.
Rawles, John
1971 A Theory of Justice. Cambridge, MA: Harvard University Press.
Sapir, Edward
1924 Culture, Genuine and Spurious. American Journal of Sociology 29:401–429.
Schroyer, Trent
1973 The Critique of Domination: The Origins and Development of Critical Theory. New York: George Braziller.
Stavenhagen, Rodolfo
1971 Decolonizing Applied Social Sciences. Human Organization 30:333–358.
Tomasi, John
1991 Individual Rights and Community Virtues. Ethics 101:521–536.
Van Dyke, Vernon
1982 Collective Entities and Moral Rights: Problems in Liberal-Democratic Thought. Journal of Politics 44:21–40.
1985 Human Rights, Ethnicity, and Discrimination. Westport, CT: Greenwood Press.
Willis, W. S.
1972 Skeletons in the Anthropological Closet. *In* Reinventing Anthropology. Dell Hymes, ed. Pp. 121–152. New York: Random House.
Wilson, W. J.
1987 The Truly Disadvantaged. Chicago: University of Chicago Press.

Lessons Learned in International Development: How Can We Apply Them at Home?

Barbara Pillsbury

I am a "development anthropologist." For more than 20 years I have lived, conducted research, and worked as a practicing anthropologist in developing countries—in Asia, the Middle East, and Africa. I speak six or so languages with varying degrees of fluency and have had considerable success in understanding and working with cultural and social issues in other countries. I have taught, lectured, and published extensively on "third world" problems and how to address them. But now I live in Los Angeles, a city larger than many countries, a city with problems far worse than many I have seen in the so-called third world.

In April 1992 I returned home after several weeks' work with doctors and nurses at an eminent medical university in Egypt. Getting into a taxi at the airport I noticed a strange smell. I asked the driver whether there wasn't something burning in his car. His answer was a shock: "What you smell burning is Los Angeles. The city's on fire." That is something I have never experienced in a "third world" country.

But even before the most destructive urban riots of this century, neighbors and other nonanthropologists persistently asked me: "Why do you need to go off to work on the problems of countries thousands of miles away? We need someone like you to focus on our problems at home."

Following the riots I became almost obsessed with wanting to fathom the complex social and cultural issues of Los Angeles (and, by extension, our nation) that had become illuminated by the riots, and wanting to find solutions. I wanted to approach these issues through the lens of anthropology and my experiences in dozens of other countries and cultures. I wanted to examine the evolving, deteriorating circumstances here to see if they could be better understood in the light of the intertwined issues on which I am asked to consult in developing countries around the world: issues of ethnicity, identity (personal, sexual, and group), immigration, population dynamics, community organization, women's status, household formation, reproductive decision making, contraception and abortion, parenting and socialization of children. As these were issues of post-riot Los Angeles, so too were they issues facing all urban America. As a visiting scholar at the University of Southern California, at the edge of South Central Los Angeles where the Rodney King riots erupted, the problems manifested were close at hand.

It is ironic, I thought, that the U.S. government pays me to consult with women in villages and towns all around the world on matters of reproduction, family planning, and birth control, yet does not ask me to consult with women in U.S. cities on these same issues.

It is also somewhat ironic, I thought, that our government spends millions of dollars guiding women in other countries to make a better life for themselves and their babies, yet never asks whether any of the lessons learned can be applied in the United States. For a long time the notion prevailed that the United States, a "developed" country, had nothing to learn from "underdeveloped" countries. But we now see shocking statistics that should make us question this premise—for example, the statistic that black men in Washington, D.C., have a shorter life expectancy than men in Bangladesh, and that infant mortality and teenage abortion rates are higher in some U.S. populations than in many developing countries.

In no other country had I witnessed the phenomenon of young mothers raising babies with so little in the way of traditional support structures. In traditional societies girls often gave birth at an early age, but they were typically in an arranged marriage and lived within an extended family where many were present to share the child rearing and participate in the socialization of the young child according to prescribed ancestral norms. All around the world, these traditional forms are slowly giving way. Los Angeles, however, seemed to have arrived at a pathological extreme.

There is one area in particular in which the U.S. government has invested far greater creative energies in developing countries than at home. This is the area of family planning and birth control, a subject the U.S. government considers a high priority for developing countries because of their rapid population growth rates. Innovative ideas and successful approaches abound.

I recall being crowded into a youth center in Mombasa, Kenya, listening to high school girls debating views on sexual activity and "responsible parenthood" (financed by the U.S. government). I remember sitting in the reception room of a Maidenform bra factory in the Philippines where the Indian manager and factory nurse described how they had added family planning to the health benefits the firm provides its employees (financed by the U.S. government). In Bangladesh I went from home to home with a young family-planning worker who also brought with her supplies for children's health and iron tablets for anemic women (financed by the U.S. government). In the West Bank and Gaza I sat in on "Life Cycle" classes with Palestinian women for whom this was a high point of their week. And I remember vividly sitting on the dry grass at a farm in Zimbabwe where a village drama team had the audience literally rolling on the ground in tears of laughter over their portrayal of a man who didn't take responsibility for his family. In those countries and others I saw many things, some that worked, some that didn't. But everywhere creative ideas were being tried (financed by the U.S. government): credit projects for women, sewing machines for mothers' clubs, comic books and rock songs with social messages, captivating videos, innovative training schemes.

This is not to argue that the U.S. government should not be assisting people overseas in such ways. In fact, the United States gives far less per capita than most other developed countries, ranking below some 15 other nations. Rather, I thought, what had been learned abroad may prove instructive for the United States. Gunnar Myrdal, Swedish Nobel laureate and author of *An American Dilemma* (1944), was not an American, yet his analysis of American society provided rare and valuable insights. The same can be said of de Tocqueville and many others. I was convinced there must be some applicability of the lessons learned in those "third world" countries to the problems of Los Angeles—and the United States.

Now some time has passed since the Los Angeles riots, but for all my efforts to turn inward and address the problems of the country to which I am native, I have not come far. I have begun working with various community-based groups in Los Angeles, helped found a new organization, the Pacific Institute for Women's Health, which shares my vision, have applied for research funding and been turned down, and recently have been approached by the Pan American Health and Education Foundation for potential collaboration in applying lessons from Latin America to the United States. I have also come to understand a great deal about how political self-interest impedes a search for solutions, and even impedes efforts to understand root causes. Thus, for example, the 1994 solution to increasingly high crime rates is to hire more police and jail third-time criminals. Who or how many are asking why we have the highest crime rates in the world?

I return to the specific area of reproductive health and, particularly, family planning and birth control. In other countries we pour millions of dollars into promoting and facilitating responsible parenthood: encouraging teens to defer marriage and pregnancy until they are older, encouraging older couples to have only the number of children that they can afford to care for. Success has by no means been 100 percent, but there has been much success in many countries. Why can we not be bolder here at home and have more vigorous and adequately funded programs to discourage teenage pregnancy, to attack the American pathology of "children having children"? Why do we not make the same effort at home as we do abroad to discourage poor couples from having large numbers of children, more than most such couples can afford to raise without the children being disadvantaged?

The answers become evident in the asking of the questions. Two important reasons stand out. First, in other countries we have the very important leverage of money. Governments in developing countries see that they stand to receive millions of dollars in grants or at least low-interest loans if they adopt population policies and implement family planning programs. Implementing a family-planning program means they get outsiders such as myself coming to provide technical assistance or to evaluate how effectively funds (especially U.S. taxpayer dollars) have been used in their programs. Often they appreciate such outsiders, who typically bring experience and lessons learned from many other countries. Sometimes they do not appreciate such outsiders, but even then they usually accept them because it is part of the "package." This is a kind of leverage that does not exist when we think of doing this type of work in the United States.

Second, when we talk about teens, especially unmarried girls, having babies too early, and think about programs to address the problem, immediately issues of racism arise. The epidemic of teenage pregnancy exists not only in black or Hispanic communities; statistics among White teens are also grim. But what politician wants to become associated with a campaign against teenage pregnancy when almost immediately he or she stands to be labeled racist?

And what role is there for the anthropologist? We may have come home from foreign cultures, those to which we are clearly outsiders. But how can we address the complex social issues, such as those that sparked the Rodney King riots, when most of us will never be native or insiders to what we see as the root causes? This remains a dilemma for the practice of anthropology.

Editor's Note. Since this piece was written, the author, as part of a group of public health professionals and medical anthropologists, has established the Pacific Institute for Women's Health. Working in partnership with the California Office of Family Planning and the Office of Multicultural Health, she and her associates have begun bringing home the experience gained from work in other parts of the world. Among the lessons learned: forging relationships with existing institutions is essential for transforming knowledge into action. Where institutions do not exist, they may need to be created and partnerships formed.

About the Contributors

E. L. Cerroni-Long is an associate professor of anthropology at Eastern Michigan University. She earned a doctorate in Oriental languages and literatures from the University of Venice, Italy, conducted postdoctoral work at the University of Kyoto, Japan, and received a Ph.D. in anthropology from UCLA. She has taught and worked as a cultural analyst in Japan, Italy, England, and North America. She is currently the chairperson of the IUAES international Commission on Ethnic Relations and is completing a book titled *American Ethnicity: The Cultural Dimension.* Her present research focus is the comparative study of Japanese and American cultures, especially in regard to education and mental health.

Walter Goldschmidt received his Ph.D. from the University of California, Berkeley, and is professor emeritus of anthropology and psychiatry at the University of California at Los Angeles. His published work includes three ethnographies on the Sebei of Uganda, several books on anthropological theory, a major analytical study of agricultural communities in California (*As You Saw,* 1947 and 1978), and a textbook developed from a series of radio shows. His latest book, *The Human Career* (1990), summarizes some of his lifelong interests by presenting a new interpretation of the evolution of social behavior in the light of human motivation. Professor Goldschmidt has been president of the American Anthropological Association and the American Ethnological Society, was a founding Executive Board member of the African Studies Association, served as editor of *American Anthropologist,* and was founding co-editor of *Ethos.*

Alexandra Jaffe served in the U.S. Army from 1983 to 1987 and received her Ph.D. in linguistic anthropology from Indiana University in 1990. Her other publications on the military experience are "The Negotiation of Meaning in the Military" (*Central Issues in Anthropology* 5(2), 1984) and "Saluting in Social Context" (*Journal of Applied Behavioral Science* 24(3), 1988). Her most recent work has been on language, identity, and resistance in Corsica, where she has been doing fieldwork since 1988. She is currently an assistant professor of anthropology at SUNY-Cortland.

Delmos J. Jones is a professor of anthropology at the Graduate School and University Center of the City University of New York. He received his doctorate from Cornell University in 1967. He has conducted research and published articles on Native Americans, the tribal people of Northern Thailand, Australian Aborigines, and the United States. His initial contribution to the topic of this collection—"Towards a Native Anthropology"—was published in 1970 (*Human Organization* 29). Among his most recent publications are a chapter in the book *Anthropology in the United States* (1987) and the article "The Culture of Achievement among the Poor: The Case of Mothers and Children in the Head Start Program" (*Critique of Anthropology* 13, 1993).

Edward Liebow received his Ph.D. in anthropology from Arizona State University in 1986. Since then he has been on the staff of Battelle Memorial Institute's Human Affairs Research Center, based in Seattle. Dr. Liebow has conducted applied research in the western United States and in South Australia, examining social networks involving urban Native Americans, and a variety of energy, public health, and social policy issues concerning indigenous communities. He edits a newsletter for the Committee on Anthropology in Environmental Planning and is book review editor for the *Journal of Political Ecology.*

Barbara Pillsbury is a medical anthropologist specialized in health, family planning, and women's programs in developing countries. Dr. Pillsbury's geographic expertise is in Asia and the Near East, where she has studied or helped evaluate health and family planning programs. Previously employed in Washington, D.C., with the U.S. Agency for International Development, Dr. Pillsbury currently heads a small consulting firm, International Health & Development Associates, established together with Soheir Sukkary-Stolba, also an anthropologist. Dr. Pillsbury received a Ph.D. in 1973 from Columbia University, where she worked with the late Dr. Margaret Mead. She was the founding president of the National Association for the Practice of Anthropology and is co-founder of the recently established Pacific Institute for Women's Health.

Mari Womack teaches anthropology at California State University, Northridge, and at the University of California, Los Angeles, specializing in symbols, methodology, and American popular culture. In her 13 years as an international radio broadcaster she has reported on news events ranging from presidential elections to earthquakes. She is author of two books—*Faces of Culture* (1983) and *Heroic Warriors: Images of the Athlete in Art, Literature and Song* (forthcoming)—and is co-editor of a third, *The Other Fifty Percent* (1993). She is a consultant and scriptwriter for the update of the anthropology TV series "Faces of Culture" and is presently engaged in writing an introductory cultural anthropology text for Prentice Hall.

The National Association for the Practice of Anthropology (NAPA) is a membership organization established in 1983 as a section of the American Anthropological Association to serve the needs of practicing anthropologists. By "practicing anthropologists" is meant professionally trained anthropologists who are regularly employed or retained by nonacademic clients, such as social service organizations, government agencies, business and industrial firms, and public educators, and who apply their specialized knowledge to problem solving. NAPA is designed to help practitioners refine their skills and market their services. It also functions to facilitate the sharing of information among practitioners, to publish materials useful to practitioners, to assist in the training of practitioners, and to support the interests of practitioners both within and outside the academy. One of the services to NAPA members is the *NAPA Bulletin*. To join NAPA, please write: NAPA/AAA, 4350 North Fairfax Drive, Suite 640, Arlington, VA 22203. To contribute to the *NAPA Bulletin*, please contact the General Editors.

ISBN 0-913167-72-X